995

I AM FULL MOON

D1158550

I Am Full Moon

Stories of a Ninth Daughter

Lily Hoy Price

Copyright © Lily Hoy Price 2009

All rights reserved. No part of this publication may be reproduced, stored in a retrieval system, or transmitted in any form or by any means—electronic, mechanical, recording, or otherwise—without the prior written consent of the publisher or a licence from The Canadian Copyright Licensing Agency (ACCESS Copyright). For a copyright licence, visit www.accesscopyright.ca.

Library and Archives Canada Cataloguing in Publication
Hoy Price, Lily, 1930–
I am Full Moon : stories of a ninth daughter / Lily Hoy Price.

ISBN 978-1-897142-38-7

1. Hoy Price, Lily, 1930–. 2. Chinese Canadians—British Columbia—Biography.
3. Quesnel (B.C.)—Biography. 4. Hoy, C. D. I. Title.

FC3849.Q48 Z49 2009   971.1'75   C2009-900983-8

Editor: Linda Goyette
Cover design: Val Speidel
Cover images: Black and white family photos are courtesy of the Hoy
Family Collection. The lantern image is from istockphoto.com
Interior images: see credits on page 173

 Canadian Patrimoine
Heritage canadien   BRITISH COLUMBIA
ARTS COUNCIL   Canada Council   Conseil des Arts
for the Arts   du Canada

Brindle & Glass is pleased to acknowledge the financial support for its publishing program from the Government of Canada through the Canada Book Fund, Canada Council for the Arts, and the Province of British Columbia through the British Columbia Arts Council and the Book Publishing Tax Credit.

Mixed Sources
Cert no. SW-COC-001271
© 1996 FSC
FSC

The interior pages of this book have been printed on 100% post-consumer recycled paper, processed chlorine free, and printed with vegetable-based inks.

Brindle & Glass Publishing
www.brindleandglass.com

2   3   4   5   12   11   10

PRINTED AND BOUND IN CANADA

To my husband, Frank,
to my late parents, who gave a bunch of kids a wonderful life,
and to my siblings, those still with me and those who wait beyond.

Table of Contents

Nine sisters shared the attic bedroom of this little house during our early years in Quesnel, BC. Our chaotic room was just large enough for three beds and a crib.

The Red Shingled House

I was born in 1930, the ninth girl in a family of twelve children. My mother gave us our Chinese names and my father gave us our English names. I was named Lily, and my Chinese name 月圓 means Full Moon. We lived in a village in a quiet valley at the confluence of the Quesnel and Fraser Rivers in the heart of Cariboo country in British Columbia. Today Quesnel describes itself as a city, but it was home to only three hundred people when I was born. Our community was at the northern end of a narrow, winding and dusty highway of dirt and gravel, eight hundred kilometres north of Vancouver. Miners and prospectors had eked out this route as they followed the meandering Fraser River during the Cariboo gold rush of the nineteenth century. I think of the Quesnel of my childhood as a Brigadoon, a village hidden in time, yet to be discovered.

My family lived in a small, shingled house until I was four. The house was painted a dark red and had a black roof. It was lodged between a corrugated tin garage and a log barn on Barlow

Avenue, a dirt and gravel street edged on either side by wooden sidewalks. A gated wire fence enclosed the front lawn, bordered by lilac bushes, and a cemented walkway led up to the porch entrance.

The main floor had a kitchen, a master bedroom with bath, and a living room. The kitchen contained a cast-iron stove, a wood box, a small counter, a round table and a ceramic sink with a cold-water tap. A door opened to a large backyard.

We had running water and electricity as far back as I can remember. However, my sister Lona reminded me that we didn't always have tap water. We had a well with a bucket just outside the back kitchen door. She helped my mother haul water to fill the kettle and the stove's hot water tank. My sister Rose remembers the well as a cool place to set a bowl of jelly. My sisters couldn't recall when tap water replaced the well, but they said we always had electricity.

The boys shared the master bedroom with my parents. It was a busy thoroughfare as we trundled in and out of the room to use the only bathroom in the house. The room contained a flush toilet, a basin, an English style tub, and a barrel heater. Once a week three or four of us girls shared a bath. Ma-mah heated a drum of water on the barrel stove. When the water was steamy hot, she poured it into the bathtub and cooled it by turning on the cold-water tap.

At bath time, the bathroom was cosy-warm and smelled

of firewood and steam—the way bonfires and wet bathing suits sometimes smell. We stripped and left our dirty clothes on the floor and stepped into the soothing, lukewarm water. Once in the tub we splashed about, wet the floor and soaped ourselves with a bar of soap. We giggled and laughed, enjoying the moment until Ma-mah said, "Okay, let me wash your hair." We hated having our hair washed and protested.

"Not me first, Ma-mah, not me first!"

"My hair isn't dirty!"

"Do Lily first!"

"No, do Mooney!"

Ma-mah said, "Close your eyes." With a bar of Sunlight soap, she lathered our hair and scrubbed our scalps as we yelped and howled.

"Not so hard!"

"Ouch, that hurts! "

"I got soap in my eyes!"

Ma-mah poured clean warm water over our heads to give them a rinse, then a quick rub with a towel. She let us play in the murky warm water even though a dark line rimmed the tub, and the film of soap suds floated and clung to us like drowned dandelion seeds. Afterwards, we stood nude by the stove, soaking up the heat and drying ourselves. We dared one another to stick out our tummies as close to the stove as possible without getting burned. The inevitable happened when Star ran screaming and crying with a scorched tummy to Ma-mah. Our daredevil game came to an abrupt end.

On chilly evenings we gathered around a small, oblong stove in the living room. Hidden behind its north wall, a narrow staircase led to an attic bedroom. We nine girls shared this attic room under low, slanted ceiling. The room had a bare wooden floor and one window, and it was large enough for three beds and a large crib. The three youngest girls slept sideways in one bed. The others occupied the other beds, except for Rose, who slept in the crib because her hands were covered with eczema that caused her endless hours of discomfort.

The attic was a noisy, crowded room without closets, dressers or drawers. Dishevelled clothes and bedding hung askew. The smell of urine permeated the thin, lumpy mattresses. A sixty-watt bulb, screwed into a ceiling socket, illuminated the chaotic scene.

In this jungle of a bedroom, I experienced my first Christmas. Our family didn't celebrate Christmas in the early years, but as a small child, I vaguely understood it meant presents, Santa Claus, and a decorated tree. My older sisters talked about it and repeated stories from school. They always told us when it was Christmas Day.

On the Christmas Day when I was three years old, I woke up shivering in the icy bedroom. My two siblings had rolled themselves into one big ball with the only feather comforter we shared, leaving me with a flimsy flannelette sheet. I pulled and yanked at the comforter, applying my feet to break apart the sleeping twosome. As I struggled to free the cover, I happened to look up. To my surprise, I focused on a sight that made my jaw drop. I released the bedding and jolted upright. Opposite the foot of my bed, slept my two oldest sisters, Avaline and May, in a white, curlicue wrought-iron bed. Little gift-wrapped packages hung from the curlicues intertwined with strips of red and green crepe paper.

"Look!" I shouted.

Eight tousled black heads, eyes like raccoons, peered out from under the covers. Their eyes followed my pointing finger, and just like me, they jolted upright in disbelief.

"Where did they come from?"

"Who are they for?"

"Did Santa come and leave us a present?"

Avaline surveyed the scene with a chuckle. She was our eldest sister with the sweetest disposition, and we looked up to her as our second mother. Whenever Ma-mah needed help, she took care of us. And when Pa-pah came close to a nervous breakdown, she quit school in Grade Eight to help him in the family store.

Unable to contain her secret, Avaline swung her feet into a pair of cloth slippers, slipped on a black and red housecoat, spread her arms and exclaimed, "Merry Christmas, everyone!"

She tapped one of the packages, which set it in motion, and said, "This is just a little something for each of you and Benny. Baby Jack's too young for a present."

A Christmas present? It was something we'd never had. I tore open my gift and yelped when I saw a box of Cracker Jack popcorn with a toy inside. "I'm going to show Ma-mah," I said, and scampered down the rickety stairs. The others followed, gesturing toward their boxes of popcorn, handkerchiefs, hair clips and ribbons, calling, "Ma-mah, Pa-pah, see what we got!"

"What is it?" Ma-mah asked, as we burst into their bedroom.

"We got a Christmas present! Avaline gave us a Christmas present! See?"

"A Christmas present?" said Ma-mah, glancing at Pa-pah. They laughed and said how lucky we were, and then wished us a Merry Christmas.

Years later Avaline confessed what she had done. "I never paid for the items I gave to you kids," she told us. "I just took them from the store."

I remember that the backyard was our playing field. Chickens wandered around it freely. Since we didn't have toys, apart from a wagon, we created our own imaginative fun. We climbed the mountainous woodpiles, splashed in a large galvanized rain barrel, built playhouses from cornflakes cartons. A deserted farm wagon

It was no easy task for Ma-mah to line us up for a family portrait. We often had to search around town and the swimming hole for missing kids. Pa-pah took this picture in the early 1930s.

f Cowboys and Indians. One day as we
ne wagon's deck, four-year-old Mooney
e her arm. For the next few days, Lona,
, who was five, sympathetically pushed
her around in a creaky, lopsided baby buggy.

Another time when Mooney lay sick with fever on our parents' bed, I felt very sorry for her. I said to my brother Benny, "Poor Mooney is so sick. We've got to make her better."

"How?"

"I know how," I said. "But we have to find some silver paper."

We searched outside until we found an empty cigarette box. I removed the silver paper, flattened it, and placed it on the surface of the hot, kitchen stove.

"Now, pick your nose and put the snot on the silver paper," I said.

We picked our noses and cooked the snot until it was dry and crunchy. Then we took it to Mooney. "Eat this and it will make you better," I said.

"What is it?"

"Just eat it," I said. "It will make you better."

Whether she ate our medicine or not, I can't remember, but she did get well.

I remember the days when Pa-pah came home for lunch after working in his general store all morning. The store and the house were at opposite ends of the block and he always entered through the kitchen. He went straight to the bathroom and locked the door behind him. Four or five of us kids crept up to the door and banged our fists on it as loudly as possible, then in fits of giggles, ran and hid. It was a daring game we played because we knew that if we were caught, we would be punished.

Pa-pah, short and stocky, appeared from the bathroom. He surveyed the empty living room and roared like a lion.

"Who banged on the door?"

No one answered. We remained fearfully hidden.

He spotted me crouched under the treadle sewing machine. He scooped me into his arms. "Oh, ho," he chortled, "So you're one of the bad girls."

"Ma-mah, Ma-mah, help me," I screamed and wiggled. He released me only after rubbing his whiskers against my cheek. I looked around. The other kids had disappeared out the door.

I remember that next to our house, on the corner, was a log barn with six stalls. A nailed-up signboard read: "C.D. Hoy. Stable. Hay for Sale." Most Saturday mornings in winter, farmers and their wives stopped at the barn in horse-drawn sleighs or wagons. The women, in heavy black coats, with knitted scarves tied round their heads, scurried off to buy groceries while the men tended to the animals. They unhitched the horses from the wagon and tethered them inside the barn, before hanging the harness on spiked posts. Once that was finished, they brushed aside remnants of snow and hay from their clothing before joining their women.

We often hung around the barn, which reeked of steamy manure and horseflesh. The horses snorted as they munched the hay and swished their tails. Sometimes we bravely patted the huge animals, while hoping and waiting to hear one farmer say, "You kids want to go for a sleigh ride?"

"Can we?"

"You sure can," said the farmer, as he lifted Benny and me onto the wagon. Lona, Star and Mooney climbed aboard. We grinned at each other as the man gave the reins a quick jerk, and said, "Giddy up." The horse trotted off, pulling the wagon with us perched happily on top.

I remember that Pa-pah made us a skating rink behind the house. For several days in sub-zero weather, with icicles hanging from his moustache, he packed the snow down with a shovel, shored up the sides, then hosed it down to create a sheet of ice. We younger kids strapped on bob skates to our shoes. The older girls wore black tube skates that bent in at their ankles. We clung to one another, screeched and laughed, staggered and fell, and got up again. Our parents watched, laughing, from the bathroom window.

I remember the summer days when we whined of hunger, as Ma-mah prepared the evening meal. "Okay, okay. Just a minute," she'd say, as she spooned hot rice from a big pot into the palm of her hand. She quickly rolled it between her palms, sprinkled it with salt and gave us each a roll, then shooed us back outdoors. It was a delicious and satisfying treat, one I still enjoy today.

And, oh, how I loved to eat fat meat. Ma-mah made soup stock by boiling a hunk of shoulder pork, skin and all, until it was tender. She then chopped it into small pieces and added it to the soup. I sat near her in a high chair at the kitchen table, as my family ate. She lifted pieces of fat meat with her chopstick and placed them on my tray. I delved into them with my fingers and gorged on the succulent morsels.

I remember watching the flies buzz and hover over the dinner table and Ma-mah and the others saying, "Shoo, shoo," as they swatted them with their hands. The creatures flitted up and away, only to be caught on the yellow fly coil, hanging from the ceiling.

I am recalling small glimpses of my childhood in the house where I was born. The little house is gone, torn down in the 1960s. I can still picture my siblings and me—chubby little kids with straight black hair, jabbering in Chinese, racing through its doors. It was not so long ago.

For the first seven years of their marriage, my parents, Chow Dong Hoy and Lim Foon Hai, lived on opposite sides of the Pacific. By 1917, Pa-pah had finally saved enough money to bring Ma-mah from China to Canada. They posed for this picture in Vancouver just before their adventurous trip to Quesnel.

Homeland

My father, Chow Dong Hoy was born in 1883 in China, Guangdong province, district of Hoy Ping, village of Sui Soon Lee. In 1902 his father borrowed three hundred dollars to send him to Canada where he might earn enough to help support his impoverished family.

In his first job in Vancouver, he worked as a busboy for five dollars a month. Unable to make ends meet, he borrowed twenty dollars and headed for the Cariboo gold fields. He arrived in Quesnel in 1903, flat broke. He bummed food from Chinese friends and thereafter took various jobs—as a dishwasher, cook, fur trader, and labourer for the Grand Trunk Railway. In 1909 he worked in the Barkerville mine for $2.75 a day. The mine closed in winter. To survive, he taught himself photography, repaired watches and became a barber. That winter he returned to Quesnel to cook in the Cariboo Hotel.

In 1910, at the age of twenty-six, my father returned to China to marry my mother, Lim Foon Hai, who was seventeen years old. My mother came from Ching Hing Lee, a village about six kilometres from my father's village. It was an arranged marriage. He couldn't afford to bring her back to Canada until seven years later. In 1917 my parents arrived in Vancouver on the *Empress of Russia*. In his unpublished journal, "History of Chow Dong Hoy," my father describes my mother's situation: "She seasick entire journey, thirty-four days. Her first time on ship. Her first time in city. Her first time away from home. Her first time on a train. Her first time she's seen me in seven years."

After two weeks in Vancouver, they headed for Quesnel. They took the train as far as Ashcroft, where Pa-pah had left his horse and buggy in care of a farmer. Somewhere on the ride to Quesnel, he stopped to feed the horse. As he unbridled it, the animal knocked him over and took off down the road with Ma-mah screaming and clinging to the buggy for dear life. This was her first encounter with a horse and buggy. Fortunately, a Model-T Ford came along and between the driver and my father, they rescued my terrified mother. And so they journeyed north for four days on the twisting Cariboo road to Quesnel and began their life together.

They had their first child, Avaline, the following year. She was the darling to all of us. Avaline was gentle and kind like our mother, and because she was the first born, my parents placed lots of responsibility on her. She took care of the younger kids when our parents were away or when they were ill or needed help. She was twelve when I was born. I can only remember her looking after us, feeding us and loving us. Like Ma-mah, she was always there. Only pictures tell me of her life when I was a child. I felt her kind and loving presence.

My sister May was born next in 1919. She was perhaps the brainiest of us all. She was very short, just four foot, ten inches when full-grown, and her height made her very self-conscious. The rest of us girls were between five foot and five foot three inches. May never participated in competitive sports but did play the piano and read books.

Anne was born in 1921. She was one of the prettiest of the Hoy girls. She lived up to her Chinese name, which meant Full of Laughter. She loved life and was popular with boys and girls.

Rose came along in 1923. She was the tomboy in the family, always into mischief, sports, and fun. She was also the most artistic one.

Yvonne was born in 1924. A chubby girl with a round face, she was rather shy and unsure of herself.

Lona arrived in 1925. She had a small, agile frame. She performed acrobatics at concerts and for friends.

Star was born in 1927. A pretty girl with fair complexion, she had a tiny waist and a brilliant smile. She was athletic, too.

Mooney appeared in 1928. She was a timid child who cried a lot due to stomach pains. Her shyness made it difficult for her to make friends when she was little.

And now we arrive at my place in the family. Silly Lily, they called me. I was a leader in play-acting, mystery tours, and games. I considered myself the Ugly Duckling amongst

When I was a child my world revolved around my sisters and brothers, and my parents. Pictured here is the whole family. Back row, left to right: Yvonne, Anne, May, Ma-mah, Irene, Pa-pah, Avaline, Rose. Front row, left to right: Lona, Mooney, Jack, Benny, Lily, Star.

the swans. We were eight swans and a duckling in the Hoy household—all girls.

On March 14, 1931, the village of Quesnel awoke to the most astounding news. Like the swoop of a swallow, the story flew through open doors and windows, through muddy streets, and beyond the farmlands. People's ears perked to listen; their mouths fell open in disbelief.

Well-wishers hustled over to Hoy's General Store to extend their hearty greetings to my father. The men tossed back shots of whisky as my father generously poured. They pumped his arm and whacked his back and called him C.D., or Charlie or Mr. Hoy. "Congratulations on finally gaining a son, after nine girls!"

No one was happier than my mother as she held her newborn. "A son," she sighed, "a son at last." She thought of her husband who had at one time suggested they stop having any more children. "No," she had said. "We must have a son. Every Chinese family needs a son." Glowing with happiness, she watched her baby suckle.

Dr. Baker, with the assistance of midwives, had delivered all the Hoy children. My parents suggested that he name the baby. The doctor was honoured to name the boy Alexander Benjamin Hoy. We called our brother Benny.

Just because the Hoy family had one boy didn't mean the family was complete. Jackson, or Jack, was born in 1933. He was a weak baby, often sick, and he remained in poor health for most of his life. He was thin and suffered from eczema and asthma and had difficulty keeping up with his siblings.

Irene, the youngest Hoy, came along in 1937. She was a sweet-natured child, but a little lonely, perhaps because she was separated from her siblings by years.

When I was a child my world revolved around my sisters and brothers and my parents. I thought of my parents as our anchor, our stability. They taught us right from wrong and made choices for us, whether we liked those decisions or not, they enabled us to know exactly where we stood in the scheme of things.

My mother was a gentle, patient woman. As I remember her in the 1930s, she always wore a full apron over a floral housedress. She was big-boned, like a farm girl, but not fat, and she looked taller than her five foot four inches. My siblings and I often followed her around during her daily chores because she always had something for us to do.

When Ma-mah planted her garden in the spring, she gave us each a little plot and showed us how to grow radishes. We dug into the cool, brown soil with bare hands and made little trenches with our fingers. Into these trenches we sprinkled tiny radish seeds from a Buckerfield's seed envelope. We covered the seeds with soil and watered them with a garden hose. When the radishes matured, we dropped them into a solution of vinegar, water, and sugar and within a day or two, we munched our own pickles. She encouraged us to help feed the chickens and gather eggs, weed the garden and set the table. In winter we helped shovel snow and in the evenings listened, terrified, to her ghost stories.

Pa-pah was a businessman, devoted to his work. He always wore a suit, a tie, and a grey fedora. He worked in his store morning, noon, and night, seven days a week, to support his growing family and to build his empire. He was a generous man who remembered his humble beginnings and therefore helped others on their way. I once saw him burn a stack of unpaid bills. "I know these people cannot pay," he said. He was a man of his word and a staunch supporter of the community.

Although Pa-pah worked constantly, he always made time for his children. When my older sisters were little kids, they liked to sleep outside in cornflakes cartons during hot summer nights. He built them a sturdy playhouse which benefited all of us. Whenever he told us he was taking us fishing at Six Mile Lake, we jumped with happiness. He plunked four or five kids into a wooden rowboat with a couple of rods and reels and a rusty bailing can. "Now, when a fish bites, reel the line in slowly and I'll net it," he said. He dipped the paddles into the glassy, dark waters. He showed us where to find clumps of lady's slippers hidden amongst the thick foliage of the damp woods. We never picked the flowers but visited them each year.

It is with pride and pleasure that I include various photographs in this book taken by my father. Chow Dong Hoy became a renowned Canadian photographer. In a way, he accidentally came upon his creative work. In the spring of 1909 he went to Barkerville to work in the gold mines. When winter came, everything froze, the mines closed, and he had bills to pay. He later wrote in his journal to his children, "No other job to be had. Make best of situation. Teached myself photography. Took pictures of [Chinese] miners. Post card on back of picture. That way two in one. Write letter and send picture."

That was his ingenuity. We don't know who taught him photography or where he found the camera. He never mentioned it and we never asked.

When he settled in Quesnel and became a merchant, he continued to take portraits of the Chinese, First Nations, and Caucasian citizens for the next ten to twelve years to supplement his income. His makeshift studios were a porch or a room near a window. Without intention, he captured history in his lens and recorded a way of life in a remote community during the early twentieth century. Fortunately, he also photographed his family and friends and his property. These family photos show where and how we lived; they document who we were and what we looked like. They tell some stories we never knew or have forgotten.

My father continued to use a camera well into his senior

years. When he died in 1973, he left behind a suitcase containing fifteen hundred negatives. They sat in the dusty basement of the family home for another fifteen years until the house was sold. We children weren't interested in them and even thought of throwing them out. I break into a cold sweat every time I think about that. Eventually we donated them to the Barkerville Museum in Barkerville, British Columbia.

This is where Faith Moosang, a graduate from the Emily Carr Institute of Art and Design, discovered them. She published *First Son: Portraits by C.D. Hoy*, a fine account of my father's life and his photography. Faith and Presentation House of North Vancouver collaborated in a touring exhibition of eighty of my father's photographs. More than 250,000 people saw the exhibit in museums, universities, and community centres as it travelled across Canada in the following seven years. My siblings and I are very proud of the historical legacy left by our father. We treasure our inheritance. The photos are permanently displayed in the Quesnel Museum, Quesnel, BC where they can be admired for their excellent quality as well as their creative content.

Had my father lived to see this day, what would he think about his unexpected reputation as a pioneer photographer? I think he would have nodded his head and said, "I am satisfied."

*We were so
overwhelmed with
the immensity of our
new house that I ran
with my sisters and
brothers from room
to room, shouting
with happiness. The
little shingled house
next door, our first
home, stood empty.*

Hoy Built

When I was four years old, we moved from our little, red shingled house into a spacious, brand new, two-storey, stucco house, where the log barn had once stood on the corner of Barlow Avenue and McLean Street. My father built the house, and it was one of the largest homes in Quesnel, measuring forty-six hundred square feet. A sign above the front porch hinted at the pride of our family: "Hoy Built."

Our new house felt like a king's castle. We ran from room to room, exclaiming and celebrating. Jumping on the plush wine chesterfields, we pointed at the imitation candles attached to the copper chandeliers in the front room and dining room. We marvelled at the two pull-out bins in the kitchen pantry that could hold one hundred pounds of rice and flour. The master bedroom had its own bathroom, a double bed for my parents, a cot for Benny, and a crib for Jackie.

As we raced up the carpeted stairway, we eyed the oak banister as a future slide. We found four bedrooms with closets, a sewing room and a bathroom with the tub from the old house. We now had two flush toilets, but the sturdy outhouse remained entrenched in the backyard for emergencies and needy customers.

The immensity of the house overwhelmed us. We must be rich to live in a house like this, we thought.

Each younger girl shared a bedroom with an older sister. Rose, who was eleven, shared the east room with me. Anne, who was thirteen, and Mooney, five, shared the north room, which had a small covered porch overlooking the backyard. On hot summer nights we often camped out on this porch, making up ghost stories. Sometimes we scared ourselves back into the house. As time passed, we used the porch to shake out rugs. In our dating years, it became a means of sneaking back into the house after our parents secured the doors. Although one or more of us girls usually conspired to unlock the front door for any wayward sisters after our parents went to bed, we sometimes forgot. When that happened, Anne, Rose, and Yvonne regained entry into the house by climbing a ladder they propped up to the porch.

I was intrigued by the silver metal doorbell—a unique device, I thought, to announce one's arrival. I soon discovered it was a weapon in disguise. Pa-pah would become annoyed when we kids slept in on Sundays or holidays—a sign of laziness to him. To wake us, he rang the doorbell, twisting the ringer until its tinny, high-pitched reverberation resounded in our ears like the booming of Big Ben. As a consequence, I still experience a twinge of guilt whenever I sleep in.

The house, known as the Hoy House, opened its doors in

1934 to the curious townspeople. They admired the intricate exterior stucco which my father described in his journal to his children: "The red colour is from the rocks packed in from Red Bluff just outside of Quesnel and carefully screened by hand. The green in the stucco is made of crushed ginger ale bottles and the amber is from smashed beer bottles. The white is marble brought in by train from Vancouver." A man named Frank Hill applied the stucco and plastered the interior walls and nine-foot ceilings on the lower floor. Harry Joyce, a local carpenter and contractor, designed the house and was paid seventy-five cents and hour while Frank Hill, received fifty cents an hour.

Visitors were amazed at the full-size basement, an uncommon feature in those days. Many homes had a root cellar below the kitchen floor, accessed by a trap door, and various types of airtight stoves heated most houses. One reason for the absence of basements surfaced in my father's brief description in his journal about the difficulties of preparing the foundation. "The basement was filled with men and shovels and was dug with scrapers, pulled by horses. A slow and big job . . . forty- by fifty- by seven-foot excavation . . . no digger machine available then."

While most people admired the house, others eyed it skeptically. They believed a stucco house couldn't and wouldn't withstand the frigid Quesnel winters and, consequently, wondered about my father's sanity. I was often asked, "How was your dad able to build a six-thousand-dollar house in the middle of the world's worst depression?" A bit of history is required to answer the question.

Apart from the availability of cheap labour, my Dad owned the property. Back in 1913 he had purchased a lot for five thousand dollars from a Chinese farmer returning to China. He used his five hundred dollars savings from the previous three years as down payment and paid the balance by instalments over several years. The property contained a barn and four or five storage buildings, one of which he converted into a retail store. With the outbreak of the First World War, his business suffered but he was able to hang on. Then came the pending threat of the Chinese Exclusion Act of 1923, which restricted the Chinese from entering Canada. My father had anticipated this restriction and had returned to China in time to bring my mother to Canada. Once settled in Quesnel, they worked and scrimped to expand the store business and to support their growing family.

Fortunately, around 1927, the Cariboo Gold Quartz Mining Company was incorporated. It went into production in 1933 at Wells, BC, a town six kilometres west of Barkerville and about a hundred kilometres east of Quesnel. The lure of gold started the second Cariboo gold rush, years after the first gold rush between 1862 and 1870 had nurtured the development of these communities. The village of Quesnel enjoyed a business boom as it served the town of Wells. Dad stocked his store with groceries,

We could not travel together with the entire family because no car could hold fourteen people. Instead, we took turns going to different places with our parents. We loved our excursions to *Six Mile Lake*, and the rare treat—a trip to *Vancouver* alone with *Pa-pah*.

hardware, clothing, guns, saddles, snowshoes, gumboots, picks, shovels, and gold pans. He purchased gold from prospectors and grubstaked others. His business prospered until he was able to expand the store in 1931 and to build a house in 1934.

On the front walk leading into the house, the name C.D. Hoy was imbedded in small, white, flat marble hexagonal stones. And in his journal Pa-pah wrote, ". . . the 'Hoy Built' sign to match the stucco was given to me. I'm proud to see so much under name of Hoy. Never expected it when I was young. I've done pretty good, never on welfare."

My father displayed his name with pride rather than with arrogance. It signified his years of hard work, frugality and determination to succeed in his chosen homeland.

And what happened to the Hoy Built house over time? After my mother died in 1964 and my father in 1973, my brother Jack and his family lived in the Hoy house until it was sold in 1982. It went through a rental and vacancy phase for eighteen years until 2000, when it was purchased and converted into a distinctive restaurant. The owners made extensive changes to the house, adding an upper deck and converting two upstairs bedrooms into a lounge area. They did, however, retain as much of the original structure as possible, kept the original chandeliers, the wainscotting in the dining room, and they left the upstairs bathroom untouched. Unfortunately, after four years, the restaurant closed and the building has remained empty for the past three years.

In October of 2006, I returned to Quesnel for a visit and booked a room at the Billy Barker Casino Hotel, an impressive structure depicting a paddlewheel steamer, symbolic of the ones that plied the Fraser River during the gold rush days. The hotel room I entered recalled the pioneer era of afghans and quilts, lumpy comforters and fat pillows, antique dressers, braided rugs on planked floors, black and white photos, old books, and floral wallpaper. "What a lovely room," I thought as I put my suitcase on a hewn wood chest and walked over to the window.

I pushed aside the lace curtains and gazed directly across the street at the Hoy Built House. I focused on the two upstairs windows that were part of my bedroom for more than twenty years. Those windows brought me sunlight, brightened my life, protected me and saw me grow from a child to an adult. I felt the windows stare back at me without recognition, and I sensed my betrayal. After the family home was sold in 1984, I had never stepped inside its doors until it became a restaurant in 2000. In the past two years I had made feeble efforts to save the house as a historical site. Lack of finances and the excuse of old age stopped my pursuit.

The windows are lifeless, fading, diminishing as the house gradually falls into ruins from neglect, and the rigid "For Sale" sign attracts no buyers. I think of my father and I'm glad he's not around to witness its deterioration. But I also notice that the original stucco remains firm and pink after seventy-three years.

The city of Quesnel wants to preserve the house as a historical site, but antiquity apparently requires the passing of a hundred years, and finances aren't available. I still have faith that the house will somehow be restored, and ultimately, chronicled in Quesnel's history. Approximately a year after my visit, the Hoy House sold on October 31, 2007, to the Billy Barker Casino Hotel. Its destiny is unknown, but the new owner is an antique buff and that gives me hope that the house will be restored and not torn down.

I write about this house because it was my home and unique for its time and place. I believe it should be honoured as a heritage home. A Chinese pioneer, a man who contributed to the town's growth, a man who left a legacy of British Columbia's history in black and white photographs, built it.

Playing on the balcony of the Hoy Built house. Back row, left to right: Lona, Mooney, Star, and Lily. Front row, left to right: Jack and Benny.

Twelve Children Under One Roof

Mealtime in the Hoy house was like a country barn dance, a hoedown. People moved in every direction. Some stomped in while others stomped out. By the time we kids had breakfast before going to school, Pa-pah and the older sisters were at work. When we came home for lunch we often grabbed a peanut butter and jam sandwich unless Ma-mah had prepared something like soup, macaroni and cheese, or stir-fried rice. We gobbled our lunches down because we were anxious to get back to the school playground. We were gone by the time Pa-pah or one of the other girls arrived for lunch. They worked shifts in the store.

We most always ate dinner together after the store closed at six. The exception was Saturday, when the store remained open until nine, and then it was shift-time again. Sometimes we sat for dinner without Rose, Yvonne, or someone else because they were late delivering groceries. Ma-mah kept food aside for them in the warming oven. Poor Ma-mah! She barely had time to feed herself. It was wonderful when we all came together. The dining room rocked with everyone talking at the same time, laughing, sharing stories, and delving into Ma-mah's delicious Chinese food.

A large family like ours had to make other practical arrangements to accommodate all of the children in the household. Our upstairs bathroom wasn't very large. The English-style bathtub, hauled over from the old house, the toilet and single basin took up most of the space. However, nine girls managed to crowd into the little bathroom or wait to brush our teeth and wash our faces. And if the lineup for the toilet wasn't too long, we stood in the hallway and shouted to the person on the toilet, "Hurry up, I've got to go!" And if you just *had* to go, then you ran downstairs and used our parents' toilet. And if you were desperate, as sometime we were, there was always the old outhouse in the backyard. We didn't like to use it because it smelled bad.

Hand-me-down clothing was a norm around our household. Ma-mah was constantly at the sewing machine or working from her sewing basket—mending coats, sweaters, stockings or sewing someone a dress. By the time coats and sweaters reached me, they needed mending at the elbows and cuffs, buttons added and patches sewn onto trousers. I can't remember ever having a new coat as a kid and it didn't seem to matter. Occasionally Ma-mah sewed me a dress for a special occasion or to replace a raggedy one. A new dress! I was delighted because I thought it made me look pretty. She made simple cotton, shift-style dresses. Occasionally she'd make us a fancy tiered or bolero-style dress, but those took longer to make and she just didn't have the time. It amazes me that from kids to adults, we never borrowed each other's clothes.

We did not travel together as a whole family. Someone always had to be home to look after the store or care for the youngest children. Even if we wanted to, the car would never hold fourteen people! Packing the car with kids was usually for short excursions into the country or to Six Mile Lake to fish and to visit the Bradshaw family, where father moored his rowboat. Only three or four of us went with my parents to visit friends in Wells or Barkerville. We took turns going to different places. Sometimes Pa-pah and Ma-mah took a couple of us to Vancouver, as a special treat.

Pa-pah and I went to Vancouver when I was about eight. It was a long trip over a twisty, dusty, gravelled road and I became carsick. My father gave me crackers to munch on to help settle my stomach. We stayed overnight in Ashcroft with friends. I remember when we neared Pattullo Bridge, just outside of New Westminster, Pa-pah said, "Look, Lily, see that bridge? Once we cross it, we'll be in Vancouver." Vancouver! I had heard that name so often but had never been there. As we drove through the city, I swung my head from side to side trying to see everything. We took a room at the Princess Hotel on Hastings Street. I held my breath and looked at Pa-pah when an elevator took us up to the third floor. Our room was wallpapered with green leaves, and there was a squeaky, double bed and an adjoining bathroom. I looked out the window at the cars and people far below. I wandered back into the hallway and stepped into the open elevator and pushed a button. The door closed and the elevator moved. I tried to open the door but it was locked. I panicked and cried and screamed, "Pa-pah, Pa-pah, where are you?" He heard my cries, realized what had happened and pushed the button back to the third floor. I was happy to return to Quesnel, and smaller pleasures.

I think the wagon was the best toy we had. It was a sturdy, brown wooden vehicle with a wooden handle, a metal grip, and iron wheels. Actually it was a utility wagon meant for the store, but we were allowed to use it whenever it was available. And that was most anytime. We pushed one another up and down the wooden sidewalk as fast as we could while the rider steered the handle and pretended it was a car. Sometimes it careened off the sidewalk and tipped over onto the gravel road, but a few scratches never bothered us.

When I was about eight or nine years old, my brother Benny and I hunted for beer bottles. We took the wagon with us as we scoured the neighbourhood streets. If we were lucky we picked up three or four. At the end of our search we pulled our little wagonload to Hoy's store and sold them for a penny a bottle. The bottles were then stashed outside in a bottle shed, at the back of the building. Sometime when we couldn't find any bottles, we took some from the bottle shed, hauled them in the wagon to the front of the store and sold them back to the store.

The few pennies we earned bought us lots of penny candy.

Every day gave us endless hours to play outside. Hide-and-seek. Tag. Shooting marbles. Playing hopscotch. And with bluebells and cockleshells in the spring air, we jumped rope to rhymes that I can still sing in my head.

Teddy bear, teddy bear, turn around,
Teddy bear teddy bear, touch the ground,
Teddy bear, teddy bear, show your shoe,
Teddy bear, teddy bear, escape do!

Grace, Grace, dressed in lace,
Went upstairs to powder her face.
How many boxes did she use?
One, two, three.

I dreamed of being a princess. My imagination created a princess coach out of a cornflakes carton with cut-out windows on the sides. I tied the box to the wagon, sat down inside it, and one of my great white stallion sisters pulled me forward. Other times we took turns riding in the box and scared each other silly by going too fast and turning too quickly on the uneven ground of the backyard. The carton usually toppled over, which created squeals of laughter as well as bad tempers full of accusations.

Other girls didn't always have a doll of their own so we shared whenever we played house. That is to say we pretended to be parents with little children. We never made our own dolls, but we did make them baby carriages out of shoeboxes. We cut pieces of material from Ma-mah's barrel of old clothes, lined the boxes and set the dolls inside. We pulled them all around the house with a piece of string tied to the front of the box.

I envied a girlfriend of mine who had every conceivable toy you could imagine. She had a playhouse in a little shack off the back porch of her foster parents' house. I often wandered over to her house to play with her many dolls, pushing them in a wicker pram that had satin pillows and coverlets. I admired all her trinkets, her music boxes and stuffed toys. But I was never sorry to go home to a bunch of noisy siblings. In the spring we consumed stalkes of rhubarb dipped in sugar. In the fall we swiped green apples off a neighbour's tree. We hid on top of a roof shed and ate the apples sprinkled with salt. At twilight we gathered and returned to our nest.

My siblings were my best friends, but sometimes we competed for the same things. From left to right: Avaline, May, Anne, Rose, Yvonne, Lona, Star, Mooney, Lily, Benny, Jack.

Almost Cinderella

Summer 1935. Dust billowed behind the McLaughlin Buick as chickens scurried away from the approaching vehicle. My father hit the horn as the car jolted to a halt in our backyard.

My sister, Avaline, now seventeen, spotted the car from the kitchen window before the honking alerted the household. She was relieved. Her responsibility for looking after the younger kids had finally come to an end. She slipped off her homemade flour-sack apron and hung it on a nail in the pantry, scooped up two-year-old Jackie and shouted, "Ma-mah and Pa-pah are home!"

Pandemonium followed. We ran in all directions.

"They're here, they're here!"

Our feet pounded down the carpeted stairway. We flew through the dining room and bolted out the back door of the kitchen.

"You're home, you're home!"

The younger children—Benny, Mooney, Star, Lona and me—pounced on the car's running boards. We flung open the doors to reach our parents and a back seat loaded with parcels. Pa-pah climbed from the car in his crumpled grey suit.

He rubbed his moustache with the back of his hand, stretched with weariness, and fanned himself with his fedora.

"Have you been good children?" he asked in English.

"Yes!" we replied in a chorus.

"Good, good." He wiped his silver-rimmed glasses with a cotton handkerchief.

Ma-mah stepped from the car, smoothed the wrinkles from her navy skirt, and brushed aside a strand of hair fallen from her bun. She greeted each of her exuberant children in Cantonese. We answered back in Cantonese because she didn't know how to speak English.

"Did you bring us something?"

"Yes, yes, of course we did."

"What did you bring us?"

"Oh, lots of good things. Just wait and see."

As we chattered, Ma-mah took Jackie from Avaline's arms.

Our parents had been in Vancouver for eight days. It was their annual pilgrimage to the coast to visit friends from China, and for my father to order various wholesale hardware and sundries for C.D. Hoy & Co. Ma-mah shopped for Chinese food not available in Quesnel. In 1935 we were one of three or four Chinese families living in Quesnel.

We eagerly offered to help unload the car. We knew when that chore was finished, the treats would come. The middle sisters, Yvonne and Rose, filled our outstretched arms with small packages. We ran into the house, dumped them on the kitchen table, and ran back for more. Rose and Yvonne carried in cases of abalone, water chestnuts, dried mushrooms, dried lily root, noodles, salted fish, and dried oysters. In the kitchen, the older sisters, Avaline, May and Anne, hauled the goods to the basement, where they filled the open shelves.

That done, Ma-mah dispensed her special treats: sesame candies, coconut toffee, preserved plums, peanuts, red ginger, almond cookies and, most unbelievable of all, sugared dough-nuts. We revelled in our windfall. Our parents never gave us extravagant gifts like blouses or dresses, nor did we expect such presents. But today, Ma-mah had a surprise for me.

In the early evening, we gathered in the dining room, eating, arguing, and talking all at once. Ma-mah joined us with a shoebox in hand.

She passed the box to me. "Lily-ah, try these on."

Silence filled the room; all eyes focused on the box. Gingerly, I removed the lid. In hushed anticipation, everyone leaned forward and peered into the box.

"Oh!" we all exclaimed.

My heart raced to the moon and back, and my eyes shone brighter than all the stars in the sky. The box contained the most beautiful shoes in the world.

"Try them on," Ma-mah repeated.

I carefully lifted the shoes, held them ever so gently, and felt their exquisite smoothness. I bent and slipped my feet slowly into the shiny black patent. A silver buckle clasped the strap across my instep. My body tingled with happiness as I stood and gazed at my feet. These shoes, these beautiful shoes, were meant for a princess. I was that princess. I stood transfixed, in a dream-like cloud, until Ma-mah's voice came to me out of somewhere.

"Oh, Lily-ah, they're much too big for you. You'd better let Lona-ah try them on."

"Oh, no, Ma-mah! Look, they're not much too big."

I quickly thrust two fingers behind my heel to prove my point.

"I'll grow into them, Ma-mah, I will! It won't take long and I'll look after them, I promise. Please, Ma-mah?"

My mother was a practical woman. The shoes did not fit. It would have been a waste to keep them. Obediently and sadly, I passed them over to Lona, four years my senior.

Her eyes brightened and a small smile crossed her oval face. She slipped her slender feet into the beautiful shoes. My heart splintered into a million pieces when she exclaimed, "Ma-mah, they fit!"

My throat tightened, my body ached. I turned from the noisy gathering. Down the basement stairs I crept in the dark. I stumbled past shelves stocked with jars of salmon, moose meat, fruit, and vegetables. I skirted by a wicker basket bulging with newspapers. Daylight filtered through two narrow, dirty windows to reveal spiderwebs clustered between the meandering air ducts and the low ceiling. The dim light guided me beyond the woodpile and around the monstrous black furnace, to the crudely cemented dugout. In the dark, on the clammy cement floor, I sat, hidden from everyone. I hunched, head upon my knees, and my tears came in big, jerking sobs.

The air ducts carried my cries throughout the house. Suddenly a light cast a faint beam into my hiding alcove. I continued to cry, ignoring Ma-mah's footsteps descending the stairs.

"Lily-ah, stop being so foolish and stop this crying."

I didn't move. I didn't look at her. Tears wet my dress.

"Lily-ah, now come out of there," she said in a gentler tone. "Come, and we'll get you a new pair of shoes from Pa-pah's store."

Reluctantly I got up. My breathing jerked as Ma-mah led me to the store at the other end of the block. We went to the shoe section where shoeboxes filled shelves from floor to ceiling. I sat sullenly while she scanned for my size. She showed me two or three different styles. Half-heartedly I tried them on. Eventually I chose a pair of oxfords—two-toned burgundy and brown with a buckled strap.

"Do you like them?" Ma-mah asked.

"Yes," I hesitated. "Yes, I guess I like them."

Years later, Lona was hospitalized in Vancouver General Hospital with cancer. One day as I stood by her bed, I noticed her foot protruding from under the covers.

"Aha," I cried, twitching her big toe. "I recognize that evil foot."

"Ouch! What do you mean, evil foot?"

"Oh, just seeing your dainty little foot, like Cinderella's, reminded me of a pair of shoes you once stole from me when we were kids."

"What? I don't remember doing anything like that."

"You don't? Well then, dear sister, let me jog your memory." I pulled up a chair and recounted the story of losing my princess shoes to her.

"Gosh, I don't remember that at all."

"Furthermore," I teased, "remember the doll incident?"

"What doll? What incident? Tell me."

"Well, I think I was about six years old. You, Mooney, Star, and I were in the kitchen feasting on bread and peanut butter when Pa-pah came in carrying a large box wrapped in cellophane. His eyes twinkled. We knew immediately he was up to something. He held the box up for us to see inside, then asked, 'Who hasn't a doll?'

"It was a beautiful porcelain doll with dark curly hair, and blue eyes that opened and closed behind thick eyelashes. She had a flawless complexion, pink cheeks, and a red mouth with

46

little protruding teeth. She wore a blue silk dress laced with tiny pearl tassels, white socks and shiny black shoes.

"Eagerly I said, 'Pa-pah, I don't have one.'

"He gave me a hesitant look, then said, 'Oh, Lily, you're much too small for such a big doll. You'll only break it. Lona is bigger and can look after it. She will give you her doll.' Well, we both knew better than to argue with him. His word was law, and thus, I inherited your old raggedy one and you got the new one.'"

"Oh, how sad," Lona said. "I don't remember either of those incidents."

"I guess I remembered them because they happened to me," I replied. "You know, for years, whenever I thought about them, I always felt a child's ache from deep within."

On a cold January morning in 1999, Lona, now free from cancer, dropped by my house in Burnaby.

"Hello, Missus! Anyone home?" She called from the front doorway.

"Come in, Lulu," I replied, using her nickname.

She walked into the kitchen wearing a knitted wool suit that accentuated her small, shapely figure. Her coiffed black hair framed a pixie face sprinkled with freckles.

"Golly, you look like a million bucks."

"Hello, Missus," she repeated with a grin. "Yes, I've been

shopping. What the hell, I might as well spend my money. Can't take it with me."

"True, true," I said. "Want a cup of coffee?"

"No can do," she said, waving her hands dramatically. "Got scads of things to do today. I just dropped by to see if you were home. I've got something for you. Be right back." She whirled out the door to her car and returned with two gift-wrapped parcels.

"For you," she said, plunking the packages on the kitchen table. "Happy sixty-ninth birthday." Before I could say anything, she kissed my cheek, turned and disappeared.

I wondered what in the devil was going on. We never exchange birthday presents. The parcels were wrapped in remnants of old wallpaper and tied with yellow satin ribbon. I carefully unwrapped the larger box.

"Oh," I gasped, covering my mouth with my hand. In the box was my beautiful doll. No, it wasn't the doll from my childhood, but that didn't matter. I took her from the box and said, "So, you've finally come home."

I knew what the second gift contained before opening it. There they were, an almost exact replica of my princess shoes. I held them, and once again felt their exquisite beauty. Overwhelmed by my sister's unexpected gifts, I placed them in the bay window of my bedroom. And a little girl rejoiced with me as I wrote a letter to Lulu.

Ma-mah called Pa-pah a "damn fool," when he replaced her cast-iron stove with a temperamental sawdust burner.

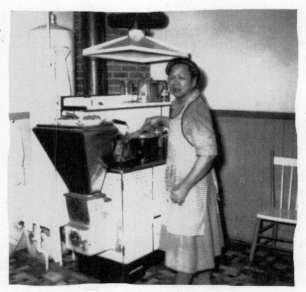

Chinese New Year

My parents celebrated the Chinese New Year but they were not obsessed with it. They couldn't afford to buy new clothes, fill the house with flowers or import expensive food for the fifteen-day celebration. They did, however, keep New Year's Day sacred. It became a household tradition—a family gathering of mutual respect and sharing. I was six years old and living in our new house before its significance became a reality to me.

It was the first day of the Chinese New Year, 1936, the Year of the Rat. In the kitchen, Ma-mah and my five teenage sisters, up since six in the morning, prepared *tay*, a kind of pastry, for this special occasion. Ma-mah chopped and minced chicken, pork, mushrooms, onions and water chestnuts together. She then passed the mixture, to be wrapped, to her daughters who were seated at the kitchen table.

They added a spoonful of the mixture onto a round, wafer-like piece of dough, folded them into a half, like Cornish pastries, and then set them aside. Other varieties of *tay*, the size of ping-pong balls, were stuffed with sweet black bean sauce, chunks of brown sugar, or encrusted with sesame seeds. All would be deep-fried like doughnuts later in the day.

When the pastries were finished, everyone rushed to tidy up—the table wiped, bowls, chopping block, utensils washed and put away.

"May, roll up a newspaper, and sweep the floor," Ma-mah said. "Don't use the broom or you'll sweep away good fortune and luck in the New Year. You know it's bad luck to do housework on New Year's Day."

"What?" Yvonne groaned and rolled her eyes. "But we've been working all morning!"

Ma-mah laughed as she wiped her hands on her apron. It bore a faded imprint of Five Roses Flour. "This is not considered work. It's preparation for a new year. Now hurry, get changed, and wake the other children."

My sister Rose poked me, threw back my covers and shouted, "Get up, get up!" She yanked the blinds. Sunlight burst through the ice-glazed windows and blinded me.

"Hurry and get dressed," she said, while brushing her hair. "Ma-mah and Pa-pah are waiting for us downstairs, so hurry!"

"Wake up, wake up," called the sisters, "It's Chinese New Year's." I heard Lona, Star and Mooney arguing in the bathroom. "I've got to go, so hurry up!" "Wait your turn!" "But I was here first!" "You've got my toothbrush!" "No, I haven't!" I rushed to join them and shivered as my feet hit the cold floor. All nine sisters squeezed into the bathroom.

"Dress carefully," said Rose. I slipped on a white, tiered dress

Ma-mah had made for me. I pulled on brown-ribbed stockings, adjusted the elastic bands that held them up and put on a pair of brown oxfords. Rose combed my hair, and then tied a pink ribbon around my head. "Let's go," she said.

At the top of the stairs we lined up in order of age while Avaline inspected us. "My, you all look so nice. Now, do you remember what you're going to say to Ma-mah and Pa-pah?"

"Yes," we nodded.

"Okay, repeat it again, in your best Chinese."

We tittered and giggled, "*Gung Hay Fat Choy*, Pa-pah. *Gung Hay Fat Choy*, Ma-mah."

To the Chinese, the words mean good luck, prosperity and long life . . . and also Happy New Year.

No one spoke as we followed Avaline downstairs, through the hallway and into the dining room. On the table was a bowl of white and yellow narcissus, symbolizing prosperity. We lined up along the wall across from our parents, who were waiting for us. Benny and Jackie, dressed in white shirts and navy blue pants with clip-on suspenders, stood on either side of our parents and watched in awe at the influx of their sisters.

Ma-mah wore a straight, grey skirt with a wine cardigan over a white silk blouse. Her hair, pulled back in a bun, emphasized her oval face and high forehead. She smiled affectionately at her daughters.

Pa-pah sported a new three-piece navy suit, a white shirt

with a stiff, detachable collar and a blue necktie tucked into his waistcoat. He watched Avaline as she walked towards him. She stood respectfully before him with eyes averted, then shook his hand, and said, "*Gung Hay Fat Choy*, Pa-pah."

He beamed at her with a smile wide enough to show a set of straight white teeth. "*Gung Hay Fat Choy*, daughter number one."

Avaline then stepped in front of Ma-mah. Showing the same respect, they shook hands. "*Gung Hay Fat Choy*, Ma-mah."

Our Ma-mah returned the greeting, and then withdrew from her sweater pocket, a small, red envelope, embellished in gold, Chinese lettering, a *lai see*, which contained lucky money, symbolizing good luck and wealth. She pressed the envelope into Avaline's hand. Avaline thanked her, then stepped back in line. May, the second oldest, came forward. We younger kids tittered and shifted from one leg to the other while we waited. The red envelope was foremost in our minds. The money it contained was a rare commodity in our frugal lives. However, we knew the rite of expressing parental respect must come first.

When it was my turn, I followed my sisters' procedure and extended my greetings respectfully. When I received my envelope, I fingered it to determine the coin's value. The ritual ended with Jackie, the youngest member of the family.

Ma-mah and the teenagers returned to the kitchen to cook

the *tay*. Pa-pah stoked up the furnace, and then went to his store. We dashed upstairs to ponder our wealth.

To our delight we deduced that each envelope contained twenty-five cents. We tucked the envelopes under our pillows because Avaline said it would bring good luck. "Maybe the envelopes are magical and will bring us lots more money," said Lona. "We'll be rich like movie stars!" As I left my room I patted my pillow and said "lucky, lucky," my mother's English version for good luck.

In the kitchen, Ma-mah and Avaline slipped onto their right arms their black, grease-resistant sleeves, elasticized at the wrist and the elbow. Into the sizzling oil they dropped rounds of *tay*, which they manoeuvred with deft flicks of their chopsticks until the pastries turned a golden brown. Then they scooped them up with a copper-meshed ladle and transferred them to thick wads of old newspaper.

When it was time to cook the puffball *tay*, Ma-mah allowed us to watch. We stood on wooden stools and peered over her shoulder. She dropped a ball of dough encrusted with sesame seeds into the hot oil. The ball sank to the bottom, and then gradually rose to the surface. Each time she pressed it down with a spatula, it grew larger until it puffed to the size of a grapefruit. We were eager to sink our teeth into the treat.

When the pastries were cooked, Ma-mah and the girls placed them on pieces of waxed paper and packed them into brown paper bags. These packages were for the local Chinese bachelors. The bachelors—restaurant owners, laundrymen, merchants, sons and lovers—were separated from their families when Canada imposed the Chinese Exclusion Act of 1923, which would last for twenty years. My mother did not forget their loneliness.

Ma-mah sent us out to deliver the *tay* within a two-block radius. "Now," she said, "Remember to address the men according to age; wish them *Gung Hay Fat Choy*, and thank them for the *lai see*. Go quickly, so the *tay* doesn't get too cold."

We struggled into our winter gear and stepped outside into brisk air and sunshine. Thoughts of the red envelope encouraged us to run through skiffs of fresh snow, which squeaked beneath our boots. Lona and Star went to the Nugget Café. Mooney, Benny and I went to the Hing Kee Laundry.

Benny knocked on the yellow painted door with its small curtained window. A pair of eyes peered from behind the curtain, and then the door opened.

A stooped, old man with sparse, grey hair welcomed us in Cantonese. "Come in, come in, my children." His eyes twinkled and he smiled at us. I saw large yellow teeth in a face marked with brown spots. We entered his room, which reeked of bleach and soap.

"*Gung Hay Fat Choy, Gongh, Gongh*," we said in Cantonese, addressing him as Grandfather, as we offered up the bags of *tay*.

"Thank you, thank you, my children, and *Gung Hay Fat Choy* to you." He shook our hands and patted our shoulders as he handed each of us a red envelope.

Out in the street, we met Star and Lona. We ran home, anxious to show off our red envelopes. "Ma-mah, we're back," we yelled, waving our wealth.

She laughed and assured us that we were very lucky children but said there were more deliveries to be made. Three more times we ran through the snowdrifts towards red envelopes that we could keep. At home we counted our windfall—as much as two dollars! Yes, we were rich like movie stars! "Put your money away or a robber might come and steal it," Ma-mah warned us.

After a delicious lunch, we spent the afternoon playing Old Maid and Fish, and listening to records on the windup gramophone. We could hardly wait for supper.

The aroma of soy sauce chicken drew us to the meal. The table was covered with a floral oilcloth and set for thirteen people—chopsticks, ceramic soup spoons and rice bowls. I saw plates of chicken, steamed pork with salted duck eggs, spareribs in black bean sauce, stir-fried vegetables, and winter melon soup with transparent long-life noodles. There would be moon cakes, and tastes to remember for a lifetime.

Our parents sat together at one end of the table. Pa-pah poured himself a shot of whisky, then offered one to Ma-mah. She brushed him off with a wave of her hand.

"You know I don't like alcohol."

"Aw, come on, just a little for the New Year?"

She shook her head in defeat, and offered her ceramic soup spoon to be filled.

"Anyone else want some?"

"No!" We scoffed at his nonsense. Pa-pah tossed back his drink with a gulp and a broad smile. We watched and waited for the alcohol to turn his face crimson.

"This tastes awful," Ma-mah shuddered between sips. "Now, eat up, before the food gets cold."

Our chopsticks flashed back and forth from one platter to the other. We inhaled bowls of rice and dipped our spoons into the common bowls of soup. As we smacked and slurped, we mumbled to show appreciation to the cook. "Mmm, so good!" "Delicious!"

After supper, everyone helped to clear the table and wash the dishes. Pa-pah had already strung firecrackers to the front porch. He would ignite them as soon as we were ready. According to a Chinese tradition, firecrackers frighten away evil spirits, and ensure good health, prosperity and happiness throughout the New Year. To us, the crackling, popping firecrackers meant fun and excitement.

We ran outside and climbed on the snowbanks, throwing snowballs, and skidding along the snowy sidewalk while we waited for the action. Soon Ma-mah arrived in her black coat.

"Stand back, Pa-pah's lighting the firecrackers," she warned.

The long extension of firecrackers, braided together by string, hung suspended on the porch by nails. When Pa-pah lit the fuse, the firecrackers exploded with bangs and flashes of fire across the front railing, up a pillar to the roof line, across the roofline, down another pillar, then to a side railing, for the grand finale—a shower of lucky red confetti on the snow.

"More! More!" We clapped and yelled. Pa-pah distributed small firecrackers to the older girls.

"You kids want to throw some?" Rose asked.

We hollered our excited answer. The girls lit the firecrackers one at a time and passed them to us. We flung them in the air, screeched at the explosion, and then begged for more. At last, we trooped back into a house full of lingering aromas.

The day closed with our traditional treat of sugar cane, tangerines and a pomello, a Chinese grapefruit. Red tangerines represented sweetness and wealth, pomellos, prosperity and status. Ma-mah collected the fruit peelings, to be dried and used as a condiment in various dishes.

Our anticipation of sugar cane set our hearts thumping; everyone erupted into frenzy when Ma-mah dispensed it. She chopped the five-foot canes into five equal lengths, stripped off the hard outer casing; split the juicy core into small chunks, then cut them into bite-size pieces. We chewed and sucked the sugary liquid, drooled and licked our lips, then spat the fibrous residue on the table covered with newspaper. Our sticky faces glowed with pleasure; our laughter and chatter rang in the New Year. I can think of no texture or taste similar to chewing and sucking sugar cane. The sweetness guaranteed a sweet year.

The day ended. I dragged myself to bed and slept, clutching a lucky red envelope.

The Secret

The house was too quiet. I sensed something wrong. My heart pounded like a drum as I listened for Ma-mah's familiar sounds: her humming, her soft words to the other kids, her cleaver as it struck the chopping block, the clatter of pots and pans. Only my sisters' subdued voices drifted up the stairs to my bedroom.

I jumped out of bed, ran downstairs in bare feet, and burst into the kitchen. Three of my older sisters sat at the table, drinking green tea.

"Where's Ma-mah?"

My sudden appearance caught them by surprise. They didn't answer.

"Where is she?"

They glanced at each other. I could tell by their grave faces and averted eyes that something bad had happened. Avaline shifted in her chair and set down her teacup.

"She's gone out," she said.

"Gone where?"

She hesitated, and sipped her tea. "We don't know."

"What? You don't know where Ma-mah went?"

I stared at them, waiting for an answer. They nervously sipped their tea and quietly resumed their conversation. Bewildered, I left the room.

My mother was missing! Thoughts of death and injury whirled through my seven-year-old mind. Would I ever see her again? I wandered through the house, searching for her. I peered into the sewing room, poked my head into her bedroom, and prowled the basement. Finally I returned to the kitchen.

Pa-pah was preparing his own lunch. I watched as he cut two slices of cheese off a slab of cheddar; heated them in a cast-iron pan and fumbled two pieces of burnt toast from the stovetop. He tossed the toast onto a plate and dribbled melted cheese over them. He poured himself a cup of hot coffee, added two scoops of sugar, spilled in some canned milk and stirred it. With his right thumb gripping the spoon in the cup, he tipped some coffee into his saucer, blew on it, and then slurped it up. He bit into his toast and cheese, chewed it slowly, swallowed, and then licked his lips.

"Where did Ma-mah go, Pa-pah?"

He continued to eat and slurp his coffee. Finally, with a glance over the rim of his glasses he dismissed me with a few words.

"It's a secret."

Secret? The word terrified me. What secret? That must mean something so awful that no one could speak about it. Suddenly, I remembered Poh Poh (Grandmother) Sing Lee. She wasn't my real grandmother, but a family friend, a stout old woman who lived alone in a one-room shack near Pa-pah's store. She sold vegetables from her large garden to the local restaurants.

She will know, I thought. Running to her house, I spotted her with a younger woman in the garden. I unlatched the gate and hurried along the garden path toward them. Two rusted four-gallon tins partly filled with urine stood under the eves of a shed. Poh Poh used the urine to fertilize her garden. Sometimes we kids peed in a pot to help her out. She used a ladle—a tin can nailed to a stick—to pour the pee around the plants.

The women sat on wooden crates enjoying the sunshine. Poh Poh waved and called out to me. "Lily-ah, come and sit and have some sunflower seeds with us."

"Good afternoon, Poh Poh. Good afternoon Auntie." I greeted them according to age in the respectful Chinese tradition.

"Poh Poh, I can't find Ma-mah. Have you seen her?"

They looked at each other and chuckled. Poh Poh cracked a sunflower seed between her crooked, brown teeth. A breeze lifted wispy strands of white hair from her forehead as she adjusted the pink eye-patch over her blind right eye. As a young farmer's wife, she had fallen from a horse-drawn wagon, and a wheel ran over her head, almost crushing her skull. She lost her eye in that accident.

"So, you can't find your Ma-mah, eh? Now, don't you worry, I'm sure she'll be home soon. Sit with us."

I shook my head as I left. Why were they laughing at me?

Walking home, I decided Ma-mah must be dead. Maybe Pa-pah had killed her and hid her body somewhere in our yard. I don't know what caused these morbid thoughts. Had I heard mother calling out during the night? Pa-pah's gruff voice? I searched for her body behind shrubs and bushes, behind the woodpile, in the sunken basement windows. Nothing. Exhausted with worry, I flopped down on the grass and wept.

How long I lay there, I don't know. Finally, I heard my father's voice behind me.

"Oh, there you are, Lily. We've been looking for you."

He appeared with my two brothers in tow. His smile and tone of voice promised hope. "Come with us," he said. "I have something to show you."

I rubbed away tears, and followed. He led us to our old house, next to our new one. The old house was empty except for the room used as a Chinese classroom for my sisters. We entered through the back door into the musty kitchen with its stained ceramic sink. The floor creaked beneath our feet. We crossed over to the living room, which now had a chalkboard nailed to a wall. Two long, lacquered desks and eight stools filled the room. At the far end, Pa-pah opened the door to what was once the main bedroom.

My brothers and I peered into the dark shadows. Sunlight filtered through the edges of a drawn blind. The room felt warm, and the smell of burning wood radiated from the barrel stove in the adjoining bathroom. Not knowing what to expect, my brothers and I huddled together, looking and not speaking. When my eyes adjusted to the dim light, I was startled to see Ma-mah lying in bed, propped up by pillows.

"Ma-mah?" I whispered. Why was she here in this dark room?

"Come closer," Ma-mah said gently, extending her hand. Her face glowed and her familiar smile and voice welcomed us. "Come, come and see your baby sister, Irene."

Pa-pah gave us a slight push forward, and we timidly made our way to the bed. Ma-mah held up the bundled creature so we could peer into her tiny face.

Benny took one look, stepped back, and gasped, "It's a mouse!"

"No, no," I said, with relief. "It's a baby! It's a baby girl!"

That was Pa-pah's secret.

I thought my eldest sister Avaline looked like a princess from a fairy tale on her wedding day. I was only seven on that hot, July afternoon, and as I watched her pose for pictures in our yard, I dreaded her departure for faraway Powell River.

A Wedding

It was a bittersweet day when Avaline married in July 1937. It was bitter for the family because she was going away and sweet for our parents to see their first daughter married. It was bittersweet for Avaline, because she married a man she barely knew, and yet, she was the sweetest of brides.

Avaline married Henry, not because she loved him but because she wanted to appease Ma-mah, who worried about having to marry off ten daughters. Ava was the oldest and according to Chinese custom, girls must marry in chronological order. She knew she had to marry to make way for her younger sisters, but first, she wanted to help our mother. Avaline was like that, always putting others before herself. She was an ideal daughter: obedient, hard-working, tolerant, giving and good-natured. "After God made Ava," said May, "he threw away her mould."

Perhaps Ma-mah had a reason to worry. Our parents would lose face if their children didn't marry. We were forbidden to date white boys, but there were few Chinese boys available in our village or nearby. Another obstacle was that the few boys we did know belonged to our clan—the Chows—which forbade intermarriage. Ma-mah need not have worried, because the reputation of the amazing family of Hoy girls spread to the farthest corners of the province. Prospective suitors came calling. One of them was Henry Sing.

Henry came to Quesnel looking for a wife. He introduced himself to our father and stated his intentions. Pa-pah found Henry to be of good character, a man of means, who owned a grocery business. My parents approved of Henry and discussed the situation with Avaline, who agreed to meet him. They emphasized that she did not have to marry him if she chose not to, nor would they ever force a match-marriage on any of their children.

A few days later, Henry returned to the store to meet Avaline. When she knew he was coming, she ran and hid under a stairwell. At the age of eighteen, she had never been on a date. Many white boys had asked to take her out, but she had always refused. She conceded, years later, "I was so dumb and shy. I wouldn't have known what to talk about anyway. I was as dumb as a pig—only a pig was smarter!"

Hidden from sight, Ava heard Ma-mah and Pa-pah call her by her Chinese name, "Ah, *Lun-ah*, Ah, *Lun-ah*, where are you?" Finally, she emerged to face the inevitable. Henry spotted her from the office and stepped out to meet her. Curious, she glanced at her prospective husband and saw a man ten years older than her, rather short, slim, not bad looking, with a crew cut and a wonky left eye. He wore a pin-striped suit.

They introduced themselves, shook hands and said they were glad to meet each other. They both felt awkward and lost for words. "I've got to get back to work," Avaline said suddenly. "I've got customers waiting." When she turned to go, Henry slipped a ten-dollar gold piece into her pocket, and said, "It's for good luck."

Avaline and Henry corresponded for a year. She never saw him again until their wedding day.

The wedding took place at home, on a hot July afternoon. Avaline wore a gown of white satin, with long puffed sleeves, a V-neckline with a lace collar. Her hair was curled in soft finger waves around her face, and she wore a pearl tiara. Her wedding attire, from Eaton's catalogue, cost twenty dollars.

Reverend Love, a young United Church clergyman, performed the service in our front room. The room was too small to hold the wedding party of eight as well as the invited guests. People stood shoulder-to-shoulder, solid as the Great Wall of China, and few could see the couple exchange their vows. Other guests overflowed into the kitchen, the dining room, and the hallway, or stood on the stairway.

Our parents wept as they thought about losing their cherished daughter, yet they were happy to know she had found a good husband.

We kids wanted to see Avaline get married, but we couldn't

see anything. We pushed into the crowd, but nobody moved. In desperation we tried to peek through the front porch window, but Ma-mah's houseplants on the windowsill and the sheer curtains blocked the view.

We had never seen a wedding, and we weren't sure what it was about. I was seven. All I knew for certain was that Avaline was going away with Henry to live far, far, away in a place called Powell River. She would have to take a ship to get there. And we heard that we might never see her again.

The thought terrified me. I depended on my big sister, and I didn't want her to go away. I didn't want Henry to take her, but she was getting married, and that meant he could. I didn't like Henry. He seldom laughed and never joked with us. He spoke quietly and politely. He was no fun, and I didn't like his wonky eye.

We kids pouted because we couldn't see Avaline get married. It was only when the wedding party took pictures outside that I saw what I considered to be a wedding. A wedding was the beautiful bride and her three lovely bridesmaids. My sister Anne, the third-oldest, was one of them. The other two were Laura Sing and Beatrice Keen, Ava's best friends. They wore gorgeous pastel-coloured gowns with matching ribbons in their hair and held bouquets of summer flowers. Avaline carried yellow roses against her shimmering gown, and her long veil spread like an open fan at her feet. She looked like a princess from a fairy tale book.

To me, the bride and bridesmaids were the crowning jewels of a wedding. The men in dark suits didn't count.

Oh, so pretty! The groom and his attendants didn't count. They were just there, dressed in black.

After the service, trays of food arrived on the dining room table. The groom's side of the family provide the feast: a roasted pig, roasted chickens, oranges, mushrooms, long-life noodles, vegetables, moon cakes, tea, sugared ginger and an assortment of candy. Guests indulged themselves heartily, drank pots of green tea and emptied bottles of whisky. Chinese guests dropped red envelopes into a bowl next to a pile of wedding presents. The house filled with merriment until it was time for the bride and groom to leave.

We followed them outside, waving and calling goodbye while we showered them with handfuls of rice. As they drove off, my siblings and I watched sadly. Tears streaked Ma-mah's face. She quickly entered the house to respond to the cries of baby Irene. Irene was only three months old and would never know her oldest sister, as I did.

Avaline's wedding is now a distant memory. My first sister continues to live in Powell River near her three children. She is thoroughly disgusted with herself for getting old and unable to serve everyone the way she used to. Arthritis slows her mobility and sometimes she's a bit forgetful, but she's still the good-natured, generous and humorous sister I've always known. The love she gave me as a child strengthened over the years and she remains my favourite sister at the tender age of ninety.

And what about the rest of the girls, and weddings? I think we turned our mother's hair grey before her time. May, the second oldest, married nine years after Avaline. Third sister, Anne, followed a year later. Thereafter, the traditional system of marrying in chronological order went to the dogs. The rest of us married when we wanted, whom we wanted and where we wanted. Three of us married Caucasians. Furthermore, we prolonged our mother's anxieties because all of us, except for Mooney, married in our late twenties or thirties. In time, our parents threw up their hands and were just happy to see us married off and on our way.

I will always remember the day of Avaline's departure. Her absence created an empty place in our hearts and in the house. However, the routine of our lives gradually overshadowed her disappearance. My sisters attended school or worked in the store with Pa-pah. Only the boys and I remained at home with mother and the baby. When we weren't playing, we helped to take care of Irene and did our chores around the house and in the garden. And every day I wished time would hurry up so I could begin school in September.

When Mr. A.J. Elliot treated kids in Quesnel to a movie at his Rex Theatre, it was a welcome break from school.

Running to School

Benny and I raced down the wooden sidewalk towards the school a block from our house. It was a bright Indian summer day in September, 1937, the memorable year of Irene's birth and Avaline's wedding. We arrived early. Since we didn't know anyone, we stayed together, chattering in Cantonese, and watching other children greet one another with hugs and howls of laughter. Not only was it our own first day of school, but it was also the opening day for the new Quesnel Elementary and High School, the place where I would spend the next twelve years.

The piercing sound of an electric bell caught everyone by surprise. The installation of modern technology astonished students accustomed to the old system when a teacher clanged a cowbell to summon attention. A teacher appeared and lined up the girls on the concrete walk in front of the main entrance. The boys lined up at the back entrance on the dirt playground. In pairs, we marched into the school. The Grade Ones led the way and the Grade Twelve students held up the rear. We climbed a flight of stairs. More teachers directed students to their prospective classrooms, each with two entrances, one through a hallway cloakroom. I learned later that the cloakroom was used not only for coats, hats and boots, but also as a detention area where exasperated teachers sent misbehaving students.

My classroom held the first two grades. Our teacher, Miss Helen Ferguson, was a young woman with auburn hair, a wide mouth and Bette Davis eyes. She welcomed us and assigned us to our seats in a row of wooden desks, each with a shelf and an inkwell. The bright room smelled new and fresh; chalkboards covered the length of two walls; a glass-enclosed cupboard held an assortment of books, coloured paper, chalk and pencils. Seven large windows faced McLean Street.

The two-storey building consisted of six classrooms, one with a laboratory; a library; a principal's office; and a teachers' room. The cement basement, separated into two areas—one for the boys and one for the girls—had bathrooms with six toilets, three washbasins and an open shower. The school brought together 145 students from one-room schools plus other classes scattered in various locations within the vicinity. One of these small schools, restored and repositioned on the school grounds, fulfilled various functions including school dances.

The school followed a ranking system according to a student's academic capabilities. If you ranked first, you sat in the front seat of your class followed by the second, third, and down the line to the person who ranked last. I competed with Lois and Pat for the first three spots. On my third monthly report card I placed ninth out of sixteen students. It humiliated me.

Thereafter, I strove to regain the top positions. How did this ranking system affect those who were unable to compete, who consistently failed and who endured giggles and pointed fingers from their classmates? It was a blessing when the ranking method was ultimately abolished.

This was also the era of the strap. I encountered it once in Grade One. On this occasion, I had deliberately elbowed Derek, the teacher's pet, and dislodged his arranged spelling pieces displayed on a piece of cardboard. He tattled. The teacher slapped my hand lightly with the strap. Never again did the strap and I meet.

When students were strapped, they stood in front of the class to receive their punishment while the rest of us watched—like a public hanging. Some stood defiant and angry, others embarrassed and passive. Sometimes an agitated teacher lashed out at a male student, striking his bare arm as well as his hand several times until they were red and swollen. Later, the school's principal administered the strap in his office. Corporal punishment (the strap) was ultimately abolished from schools in 1973.

I think I was in Grade Three when we were taught the MacLean method of handwriting. We learned to write with our whole hand and not our fingers. The end result was a graceful, legible style of handwriting. We practiced with a pencil to make rows of ovals within two lines and perfected the alphabet with sweeps and turns. We then advanced to a glossy red, wooden pen, sculptured to fit the hand, and dipped its steel nib into the inkpot on the right-hand side of our desk. The nib made scratchy noises and dripped inkblots as we wrote and re-wrote, "The quick brown fox jumps over the lazy dog," a phrase that uses every letter of the alphabet. We blotted the excess ink with an array of coloured blotters, which we collected like kids today collect hockey cards, except that our blotters were free, compliments of the local merchants.

My years in elementary school tumbled by. We always seemed to have something to laugh about in the classroom. One day after lunch I returned to my classroom and headed for my seat. I noticed an upturned can the size of a five-pound lard pail sitting on my desktop. I noticed, too, a piece of straw sticking out from underneath. That made me suspicious. I took another seat. I said to the boys who were watching me, "Okay you guys, what are you up to?"

"Up to?"

I could tell by their sheepish grins that they were up to no good. Just then the bell rang. George quickly flipped the can over, picked up a fourteen-inch garter snake and dropped it in the container. All the girls screamed. George put the can on the teacher's desk. When Mr. Clark entered, he peered into the container, smiled and continued with his lesson as if snakes were perfectly acceptable in class.

I became an avid reader at school. At home, our only

leisure reading came from comic books and the comics in the newspapers. We looked forward to the weekend edition of the *Star Weekly* and *The Vancouver Sun*, which contained a pull-out section of comics. I don't remember having any children's books in the house. My mother didn't read English and my father, only a little. There weren't any libraries or bookstores around. We were encouraged to read the series of books given to us in school—*Taking the High Road to Reading, Writing and Listening*, I think they were called. I discovered the wider world of books when I read a collection of fairy tales at my friend's house. One story was about an elf living in a mushroom house in the forest. I've never forgotten the glossy cover with its illustration of an elf sitting amongst ferns and mushrooms with red polka-dot roofs. After that I sat at home by one of the hot-air vents for hours reading books from the school library. I liked all kinds—especially sad and dramatic stories like *Little Women*. Books took me into a world of imagination and developed a new sense of my creativity—to paint, to write and tell stories. I also liked to read and memorize poems such as "The Raven," by Edgar Allan Poe, "I Wandered Lonely as a Cloud," by William Wordsworth and "The Rime of the Ancient Mariner," by S.T. Coleridge.

My later school years coincided with the Second World War. I couldn't understand the significance of the war as a child, but it frightened me when I heard my parents and others say that Germany had gone to war. War was also a topic of conversation in our house because my father hated the Japanese for invading China in 1931. I remember whenever an airplane flew over Quesnel, we ran outdoors to look up at it, and we immediately related it to the war. It was unusual for us to see planes in those days.

In school we purchased war stamps to raise funds for the war effort. I think they cost twenty-five cents each and we stuck them in a folder until it was filled. Also, in school we were taught to knit white face cloths for our Canadian soldiers overseas. Our teacher, a devout and patriotic Englishman teacher, encouraged us to sing, "There'll Always Be an England," and "White Cliffs of Dover," at least twice a week. War movies were popular, mostly American propaganda. We lapped up the message and hated the Germans and Japanese as instructed. When Canada interned the Japanese Canadians in 1942, Chinese Canadians wore a "China" brooch on their clothes so there would be no confusion. I didn't know of any Japanese living in Quesnel at the time.

At school my horizons broadened as I embraced Caucasian friends, the English language and culture. At one point I envied my friends' English noses and clipped on a clothes peg to enhance my flat nose. Overall, I did not experience racial discrimination. Some schoolmates and I called each other names during a quarrel but remained friends after the spat. Later, in high school dramas, I played Caucasian roles without raising eyebrows. As a teenager I sometimes resented my ethnic identity and wished

I were white, but I didn't dwell upon it. Life overflowed with adventure, promises, friendship and the future. My only regret was that I gradually lost my own language.

I can look back on my school days as a glorious adventure filled with vitality and friends with whom I've stayed in contact throughout the years. My old school still stands, although its structure is somewhat modified. The town renamed it the Helen Dixon Elementary School in 1965 to honour my Grade One teacher, Helen Ferguson, who taught school in Quesnel for thirty years. The school is now used for community services.

*My brothers Benny
and Jack did their
best to behave
themselves at
Christmas time.*

A Christmas Story

One Saturday afternoon during the Christmas holidays, Benny and I sat around the house feeling bored with nothing to do.

"Let's go over to Pa-pah's store and look around," I said, as I pulled on my jacket without buttoning it. "Maybe we can find something to do there."

"Okay," Benny said. "Maybe someone will give us some candy, do you think?"

The snow banks glistened in the slanted sunlight as we slithered down the path that led to the back of the old, log store. We stepped into the hardware section and slammed the door. The sudden gust of air set in motion whisk brooms, can openers, ladles, funnels, egg beaters and other sundries, all suspended from the ceiling. We scurried past the cast-iron stove, crackling and spitting sparks, past kegs of nails, and shelves filled with hammers, pots and pans, as we headed for the passageway that led into the new store.

The new building was divided into dry goods on the left, and groceries on the right. On the grocery side, we saw shelves and bins from floor to ceiling. A stem of bananas hung above open boxes of oranges and apples. My sisters worked behind a long counter painted blue and orange. They scribbled down customers' orders in sales books, added up the costs mentally, then checked them on a bulky adding machine. Once the orders were filled, they were boxed and set aside for delivery. They packaged bulk foods—raisins, prunes, dates—into cellophane bags, and used machines to slice slabs of bacon and grind coffee beans. And every Christmas season, they helped Pa-pah tag and deliver frozen turkeys to long-time customers and a Christmas cake to others.

In the dry goods section customers could find shelves of fabric, Hudson's Bay blankets, shoes and clothing for men, women and children. Glassed-in counters held chinaware, wallets and watches. Ladies' blouses and dresses hung above a counter along a metal bar, and sisters Rose and Anne used a long-handled hook to take them up and down.

The store was decorated for Christmas. Benny and I gawked at the red and green streamers looped across the ceiling and poked our noses near the sprays of evergreens that smelled like the woods in summer. We giggled when customers greeted us.

"Christmas will soon be here," I said to Benny. "Let's go to Pa-pah's office and write a letter to Santa and tell him what we want!"

"There's no Santa. The kids at school told me. It's only Pa-pah."

"I know, I know, but let's just pretend. Just for the fun of it, okay? Look, there's lots of paper on Pa-pah's desk."

As we pulled chairs up to the desk, I wondered: Was there or wasn't there a Santa Claus? I had seen him with my own eyes at Mooney's school party a couple of years before, but my friend Patsy told me he was only a pretend Santa. Even so, last Christmas he had left money envelopes on our tree for everyone—even for Ma-mah and Pa-pah. So, there must be a Santa.

With stubby pencils and slips of paper, we wrote our letters.

"Dear Santa, I want a ball for Christmas," wrote Benny.

It was my turn. "Dear Santa, I want a doll for Christmas."

We sounded each word aloud as we wrote and rewrote our letters on several pieces of paper. Suddenly, Mooney poked her head into the office and yelled, "Supper's ready!" We dropped everything and ran out of the office. We left our letters scattered over Pa-pah's desk.

"Close the door," said Ma-mah, as we crashed into the kitchen.

"What's for supper?" We kicked off our boots, and tossed our coats on top. The wonderful aroma of her food always made us as hungry as wolves.

We lined up as Ma-mah scooped us each a bowl of rice. We dipped our spoons into the common soup bowl and slurped its contents. Nobody talked as chopsticks clicked into the main dishes of stir-fried vegetables and steamed pork with salted fish. Nobody talked as we wolfed down our rice. Nobody said a word until Benny said, "Oops," and dropped his bowl, spilling rice onto the floor. Everyone burst out laughing and accused him of being clumsy.

Two weeks earlier, Pa-pah had trudged through deep snow in the woods, and chopped down a spruce tree. He left it in a shed until the icicles melted and the limbs thawed. When he brought it inside, the tree touched the nine-foot ceiling in the front room. Tonight, four days before Christmas, our five older sisters would decorate it. The rest of us cavorted about singing, "Jingle Bells" and "Away in a Manger."

"You kids stay out of the front room while we decorate," said bossy Rose.

"Aw, we want to come in and watch."

"No, you kids stay out. When it's ready, we'll open the door, and it will be a surprise for you."

"Please, please, let us come in. We'll be good, we promise!"

"No," she said, and locked the door from the inside. She even hung a dishtowel over the glass doorknobs so we couldn't peek through the keyhole.

In desperation we rushed outside onto the snow-covered porch to peer through the window, but she had pulled the blinds right down. We moped about the house and complained to Ma-mah of unfair treatment. She just told us to go and play.

At last we heard, "Okay, you kids can come in now."

We pushed and shoved in front of the door. Rose unlocked it and we entered a room in total darkness. Suddenly the tree lit up and glowed red, green, blue and yellow. Silver streamers glittered, dangling glass balls sparkled, and the strings of pink popcorn we had strung last year, danced from limb to limb.

"Oh, it's so beautiful," we gasped.

It was a long four days to wait for Christmas. Wrapped gifts gradually appeared under the tree. We squeezed, pinched, shook and smelled them, and we squealed with delight whenever we found our name attached to one or two. On Christmas Eve, Ma-mah said, "Christmas morning comes early," and shooed us to bed.

From my bedroom I heard Ma-mah and my older sisters in the kitchen preparing Christmas dinner. I also heard Benny toss and turn in his room. I slipped out of bed and poked my head inside his door.

He looked wide-eyed at me and whispered: "Can't you sleep either?"

"No, I can't. Let's go and look at the tree, okay?"

"Okay."

We sneaked downstairs and quietly entered the front room, closing the door behind us. The room glowed under the Christmas lights. We knelt beside the tree and poked at the presents. Poke, poke, poke, looking for Benny. Poke, poke, poke, looking for "Lily." I poked a surprising present. "Look, Benny! You've got a present from Santa. Look, the card says, 'To Benny from Santa.'"

Giddy with curiosity and excitement, I said, "Let's take it to your room and open it. We'll put it back later and no one will know!"

I grabbed the package, and we scampered to Benny's room and shut the door. We leapt up on the bed and carefully removed the tape and several layers of old newspaper. And there it was, a ball!

It was an old sponge ball. The painted stripes of red, white and blue were faded, peeled and pock-marked. Bits of the sponge were gouged as if chewed by a dog.

We looked at each other, then burst into uncontrollable fits of laughter. Benny buried his face into his pillow while I covered my mouth with his blanket. Our bodies shook as we smothered our laughter.

"Pa-pah must have read our Santa letters on his desk," I whispered.

"Well, I got my ball," Benny chuckled, then doubled over again into his pillow. "We'd better put it back before Pa-pah finds out."

"Okay," I said, reaching for the heap of newspaper. I carefully re-wrapped and re-sealed it. Somehow, it didn't look quite the same. We slipped it under the tree and buried it beneath a pile of presents. Back in bed, I giggled at the thought of Pa-pah reading our letters and the joke he played on Benny. And at last I knew that Pa-pah and Santa were the same magical gentleman.

If a child has never experienced the joy of living and playing in snow, they will have missed a wonderful part of life. I was blessed to grow up in Quesnel with its beautiful winter season. I remember winter fun with sisters and brothers, Ma-mah's nourishing winter foods and how good a scoop of snow tasted from a wet mitten.

Snow, beautiful mounds of snow, sometimes icy, sometimes soft as a cloud, sometimes sticky and wet—always inviting, always a playground. Snow kept me outside, it kept me inside. It made me laugh, it made me cry, it enhanced my childhood. Every year when the first snow fell, we rushed outside with squeals of laughter, opened our arms, lifted our faces, and stuck out our tongues to catch the delicate flakes. The snows began in November and continued to fall for the next three to four months.

Winter in Quesnel usually offered blue skies and brilliant sunshine and the temperatures hovered between minus ten centigrade and minus twenty. It was a dry cold unlike the damp and chilly season typical of other regions of British Columbia near the ocean. Occasionally the temperatures dropped as low as minus thirty or minus forty for three or four days, and sometimes a blizzard blew in with whipping pellets of snow. Those were the times we remained indoors.

One winter morning when I was about seven or eight years old, Benny, Mooney, Star, Lona and I sat in the kitchen eating our bowls of porridge. In winter Ma-mah always fed us hot oatmeal, covered in white sugar and canned milk, to keep us healthy and warm. As we gobbled down our last spoonfuls, she said, "It's a beautiful day. You kids should go outside and play."

I looked out the back window as I sipped a cup of hot Chinese tea from Ma-mah's teapot. It had snowed during the night and our backyard looked like a fallen cloud sprinkled with stardust. Snow banks along the pathways towered upwards five or six feet, and Pa-pah was outside shovelling snow.

"Let's go and help Pa-pah shovel," I said to the others.

We pulled on snow pants, put on wool coats, tugged on boots and found hand-knit toques and mitts made from various coloured yarns. We ran outside. The crisp, cold air and invigorating sunshine made us leap and holler just to be alive, and we squinted from the glare of white snow. Pa-pah had already shovelled the light, dry snow from the pathways of the house to the store and from the chicken house to the garage. He was about to clear the pathways to the woodpile and flour warehouse.

"Can we help you, Pa-pah? Can we shovel the snow too?"

Pa-pah leaned on his shovel, tilted back his fedora, and

grinned. "No, no, it's almost finished. You run along and play."

We scrambled up the snow bank and slid down on our bums, which created more snow for Pa-pah to shovel.

All morning we played in the snow. We made a snowman who wore one of Pa-pah's old hats and a knitted scarf of many colours. We built snow forts and had a snowball fight. We chased one another in a game of Fox and Geese and when we were tired, we flopped on our backs to create snow angels.

"Look at those icicles," Benny said, pointing towards the garage.

We stood on a snowbank and broke off the longest and thickest icicles hanging from the eves of the garage. We sucked the frozen, sweet waters, then bit off chunks and crunched them between our teeth until the liquid drooled down our chins. Our water-soaked mittens, clustered with tiny snow-pills, numbed and reddened our hands. Our chins and mouths chapped and stiffened. Our feet were frozen, but we didn't care.

"Lunchtime!" Ma-mah yelled from the back porch.

We raced to the door. On the porch we stomped the snow off our feet and wiped them on a coco mat. Ma-mah whisked away any snow clinging to us with a corn broom. As she swept the porch we ploughed past her into the warmth of the kitchen, then stumbled down into the basement to remove our wet clothes and to put on dry ones. We hung our coats and pants on a rope clothesline that drooped in the middle. We wrung out woollen mitts and stretched them, to prevent them from shrinking. They stunk like boiled mutton.

Back in the kitchen we scrambled for position in front of the stove to keep warm. Shoving, pushing and arguing, we spread our cold hands out towards its hot surface. The aroma of soup in the large aluminium pot made us ever so hungry.

"Sit down and stop your squabbling," Ma-mah ordered and gently pushed us away from the stove. She stoked the fire with a poker then replaced the lid over the flickering flames. We sat on roughly hewn stools painted a light green. The homemade table painted the same colour had a white oil cloth.

Ma-mah hummed as she added a dash of soya sauce and a few drops of sesame oil to the soup and gave it a stir. She took a sip and gave a nod of approval. She filled our bowls and said, "Be careful, it's very hot."

We stirred the thick soup and blew on it to cool it down. This was no ordinary soup. It's called *juke* or *congee* or Chinese-style turkey soup. It remains my favourite.

This is how Ma-mah made it:

She boiled leftover turkey bones with about a cup of rice, a chopped onion or two, a piece of dried tangerine peel, salt and pepper. When the meat fell away from the bones and the rice became a thick gruel, the bones were removed (and we were allowed to lick them). She then added a few slices of black, dried mushrooms, a bunch of salted turnip greens and a sheet or two of dried tofu, all previously soaked and softened. The soup is returned to the fire to simmer for about thirty minutes until all ingredients are blended and cooked to the point of delicious. Optional: soya sauce and sesame oil. This was the taste of winter in Quesnel.

What about those winters days when the sky remained overcast and the snow fell incessantly? On these dark and gloomy days we stayed indoors.

We girls went to school bundled up in wool coats, wool sweaters and wool skirts. Trousers were forbidden. Instead, we wore underwear, a pair of navy bloomers called knickers, made of cotton fleece. The elasticised legs reached the thighs and covered the elastic bands that secured brown, ribbed stockings.

School in winter was acceptable because there was always something to do there with friends, but weekends and holidays could drag on and on. Some mornings I slept in just to keep warm. The heat vent in my bedroom produced little if any hot air. Even though Pa-pah fired up the cast-iron furnace in the basement, night and day, the house remained chilly because it wasn't insulated. Storm windows were attached to the windows, but still, the cold seeped in and Jack Frost scrawled his art over the windowpanes.

Later in the day, we had fun with packets of well-worn Bicycle brand playing cards. We played games of Fish and Old

Maid, or we stacked the cards one on top of the other to build box houses, and when someone knocked them over, arguments erupted and tempers flared. We also played house in the dining room. We draped sheets and blankets over chairs and the table to create a tent-like house. Inside we sat on pillows and cushions and served Chinese tea and crackers smeared with peanut butter and jam.

My specialty was to get a couple of kids to perform a play, a song or a dance with me as leading lady. Mother's barrel of old clothes and rags yielded excellent costumes. My captive audience of siblings always laughed and clapped. Other times we cranked up the gramophone in the front room and danced or acted silly. The kitchen was the hub of the house, always warm and cosy in winter. We gathered around the old woodstove with its embracing warmth and lingering aroma. I loved the whiff of burnt wood and smoke, the sound of crackling and snapping wood, the sight of a flashing red, orange and blue flame from an open lid. And added to this comfort zone were the cups of hot cocoa and big pans of toasted, buttered crackers Ma-mah made for us.

The kitchen stove was connected to a tall, slim water tank which added to the kitchen's warmth. However, the tank wasn't large enough to supply us with the hot water we needed. Sometimes we used hot water from the stove's storage tank just to do the dishes. To have a hot bath, you had to be home at the right time and then, the tub was only partially filled. We just got used to having a quick warm bath in a cool bathroom.

If winter stayed too long with freezing temperatures and dark, depressing days with nothing to do, our temperaments became as ugly as the weather. Our caged energy erupted in fights and arguments. Ma-mah sometimes shooed us outdoors just to keep her sanity. Sometimes we wandered over to Pa-pah's office to amuse ourselves, hoping a candy salesman would be there to display his goods for Pa-pah. We lingered by the office doorway until the man gave us each a chocolate bar to get rid of us.

Snow fell throughout February and sometimes March, and by then, we wished it would go away. We hated our winter clothes and shrunken mitts. We yearned for the warmth of sunshine, the perfume of lilacs, the sight of buttercups and the wonderful fresh smells of spring.

Benny and Jack are
ready to go berry-picking
on a hot summer day.

Buttercups, Strawberries and Blueberries

Buttercups. When spring arrived in Quesnel, my siblings and I were jubilant. Our energy soared with the sunshine on our shoulders, and the long hours of daylight. We ran through mud puddles, floated paper boats on streams of melting snow, picked pussy willows and stopped bickering and fighting like caged animals.

The hills and valleys turned green and sprouted pockets of blue violets, white field chickweed, pink shooting stars and yellow buttercups. For kids in Quesnel, buttercups meant that spring had officially arrived. Each spring, Pa-pah religiously drove us to see the buttercups in bloom. Each spring was as exciting as the spring before, and the first buttercup sighting always happened on a sunny day.

Six or seven of us would clamber into the car and jostle for a window seat. Along the way we sang in a chorus, "Buttercups, Buttercups," loud and long. The noise must have driven Pa-pah slightly mad but he cheerfully drove the car along the gravel road to our destination—Two Mile Flat. As we neared the area, we hung out the windows, determined to spot the first buttercup. Flailing hands and fingers pointed towards a sighting.

"There's one! I saw the first one!"

"No you didn't! I did!"

When Pa-pah parked the car, we flew like bees into an open field flamboyant in yellow as far as the eye could see. Invigorated by fresh air and beauty, we ran, skipped, twirled and laughed amongst the blooms. "Buttercup, Buttercup, Buttercup," we shouted to see who could say it the fastest. Our voices reached the sky, the hills, and meadows. We called to one another and to no one.

We pulled up fistfuls of the short-stemmed flowers; their waxed petals glistened in the sunshine like butter. Pa-pah watched us from the outskirts of the field. "Pa-pah!" we yelled, as we raced towards him. We thrust bunches of the uprooted buttercups beneath his chin. If his chin reflected the colour yellow, it meant that he liked butter.

"You like butter," we chanted and teased.

"No, no," he laughed. He shook his head and said in broken English, "I no like butter, this the colour of my skin!"

"No," we protested. "You like butter!"

Strawberries. I remember Quesnel summers as hot, dry and dusty. We lived downtown on the corner of Barlow Avenue and McLean Street—two gravel roads. Passing vehicles and arid winds churned spirals of dust that settled on our lawn, on the porch and inside the house. Hiding from the heat and dust, we would loll on the cool linoleum floor playing with decks of old cards through a summer afternoon.

The scorching month of July was the perfect time to pick wild strawberries. When Ma-mah announced it was time to pick berries, we groaned and whined. "Aw, do we have to? It's too hot outside." She ignored our moans and grunts and handed each of us a three-pound Burns lard pail with a wire handle.

"It's cool this morning," she said. "It's best to go before it gets too hot." She herded the two boys and four girls into the car. Pa-pah drove us back to Two Mile Flat, to the opposite side of the buttercup field, which was now brown and overgrown with clumps of clover. He dropped us off and then returned to town. We followed Ma-mah across an open field to a grove of trembling aspens. In the shade of the rustling silvery green leaves, she spread a blanket with a West Coast Native design. She put down a cardboard box containing our lunch.

After we had cushioned the bottom of our pails with thimbleberry leaves, Mother led us to an abandoned railway track. Along its rails and between its ties grew clumps of strawberry plants clustered with sweet-scented red berries.

To fill a three-pound pail with tiny berries isn't easy, especially since we put more berries into our mouths than into our pails. We concentrated on our chore. The sun scorched the places on our necks that our straw hats didn't cover. We stood and fanned ourselves, hoping to catch the breeze that fluttered through the aspen leaves.

As time dragged on, we began to grumble. We were *dying* of thirst, of hunger, of fatigue. Ma-mah calmly assured us that we would soon be finished and encouraged us to continue. "Look at all these berries! Come and get them." She would find one cluster after another, adding a handful to each of our pails. Only when the sun hit its zenith did she call to us. "Okay, it's time for lunch."

We flopped down on the shaded blanket or leaned against the aspens' smooth, white bark. We devoured peanut butter and jam sandwiches and drank cups of hot green tea. Ma-mah fanned her flushed face with her straw hat and warned the boys to be careful as they chased a rabbit. We girls lay on our backs and watched fluffy clouds slowly drift and change into different shapes. We wished Pa-pah would hurry and come for us.

"Here comes Pa-pah," Mooney shouted, waving her hands to attract his attention. We jumped up, grabbed our pails, and hightailed it across the field to meet him.

"Look Pa-pah, see how much I've picked!"

"Do you want some, Pa-pah?"

"Are we going home now, Pa-pah?"

The summer-sweet aroma of strawberries soon filled the house. Mother removed bits of debris from our pails, and then topped them with her berries. "Now," she said, "take them to the Nugget Café, and they will give you twenty-five cents a pound for them."

Looking like street urchins covered in berry stains, we trotted off to the back door of the café. The Chinese men gathered round to praise our efforts. They gave us scrumptious cones of strawberry ice cream, made in a sawdust shed on the premises. On our way home, we savoured our treat with long sweeps of our tongues. Our coins jingled in our pockets.

Blueberries. The heat intensified in August. In the evenings, doors and windows remained open. We slept in our skivvies. In this sultry season, wild blueberries grew plump and ripe for picking.

When we picked berries on a Sunday, a couple of my older sisters would join us. They loaded the trunk with extra pails and shallow cardboard boxes. As many as ten of us piled into the car. Pa-pah drove us about seven kilometres south of the village, to the edge of the deep woods. Sometimes he stayed with us, but most of the time he returned to work.

Ma-mah located a site near some fallen logs and tied a white rag onto a tree limb to identify the spot. The lunch box, blanket, boxes and extra buckets were left there in the shade of the giant evergreens. The older sisters, with three younger ones, wandered off in search of berries. Ma-mah warned them as they left: "Don't go too far. Make lots of noise to scare away the bears." My two brothers and I went with Ma-mah into the woods. Shrubs of Oregon grape snagged our clothes; we tripped over dead stumps, and struggled over fallen logs crawling with ants. Finally we came to a clearing carpeted with shrubs laden with the bluest of berries.

"Oh, look at all these big ones," Ma-mah said, lifting up a stem. "Come and get them."

We squatted near her and gobbled up fistfuls before adding a few berries to our buckets. Ma-mah hummed as she picked. Occasionally she stood, stretched her back, looked around, then cupped her hands to her mouth, and hollered, "Yooo-hooooo!"

Immediately, the older girls echoed back, "Yooo-hooooo!"

Knowing all was well, she returned to her tasks: picking berries, listening for bears and watching over her kids. She had not forgotten the time when I was about three and was left behind in the woods. Driving home she noticed my absence and exclaimed, "Where's Lily?" Pa-pah made a quick U-turn. "Everyone stay in the car!" they ordered. "We don't want anyone else getting lost." They ran into the woods calling my name until my cries were heard. Pa-pah scooped me up and carried me back to my waiting family.

Apart from being frightened, I can't remember what happened while I was lost. My sisters said, "You told us you found a toilet and used it, and that you saw a bear and hid until it went away. Boy, what an imagination!"

When our blueberry pails were full, we carried them to the marked spot and dumped them into the boxes. Off we would go again in search of another clearing and pick, pick, pick.

Before long, my brothers and I would complain of being tired and hungry. Since we were little, Ma-mah allowed us to chase squirrels and butterflies and poke at anthills.

At lunch time, she called the others. She took Jackie's hand and led us back to our stash. At the stash, my older sisters had left buckets of berries heaped to the brim. My half-filled bucket looked pathetic beside their pails, so I cupped handfuls of their berries into mine. Just then, Star came crying and limping with one running shoe soaked in blood. She had jumped from a log and landed on a sharp twig. Ma-mah quickly removed Star's shoe and sock, wrapped a rag around her foot, grabbed some leaves off a bush, masticated them and applied the poultice over the wound, which stopped the bleeding. Another time Star had picked a poisonous mushroom and stuffed it into her mouth. Fortunately, Ma-mah saw her do it and forced her fingers down Star's throat to remove the fungus and make her vomit.

During lunch break we relaxed on the blanket or propped ourselves against logs to eat our sandwiches and cookies and to sip cups of green tea. After five or six hours of berry-picking, the food was gone, the containers full and we waited impatiently for Pa-pah to pick us up again.

Back home, we cleaned the berries and sold them to the Nugget Café for ten cents a pound. The money we earned was ours to keep. The wearisome day of berry-picking was forgotten with the first taste of Ma-mah's flaky blueberry pie.

Whenever we look back to our youth, my siblings and I realize that berry-picking was an important part of our lives. Today, our freezers are filled with blueberries, raspberries, strawberries and blackberries. However, apart from picking wild blackberries, we now go to U-Pick places on cultivated berry farms. We miss the serenity of the scented forest and we miss the open fields and a sense of freedom that we found there. We are grateful to our parents for making us pick berries in summer—it taught us patience and discipline, and an appreciation of nature's bounty and beauty. Unfortunately, our childhood berry bush habitats are gone. They've been destroyed by logging or turned into housing developments, and I can't help but lament the encroachment of civilization.

*Bridges across the
Fraser and Quesnel
River led to a village
that will always linger
in my imagination as
it was in the 1930s,
no matter how much
the city changes in
a new century.*

The Three Bridges of Quesnel

I like to remember my hometown as it was in 1939 when I was nine years old. Perhaps my childhood friends, now in their late seventies, see the same Quesnel as I do when they close their eyes.

From the top of Red Bluff hill, we can see the valley of sprawling farmlands surrounded by hills of dense evergreens and lush forests. The village is nestled at the junction of the Fraser and Quesnel rivers. From this high point, we can see three picturesque wooden bridges: two of them span the swift, clean and clear waters of the Quesnel River, and the third crosses the muddy waters of the Fraser River. These three bridges are the arterial highways of my life.

The first bridge is the Quesnel Bridge, the southern entrance into the village. The road takes us along relatively wide, gravel streets and clusters of mainly small painted wooden houses with brick chimneys, picket fences and gardens.

A short walk from the bridge, along Carson Avenue, and we can see my school, the Legion Hall and the United Church with a graveyard behind it. The street takes us past the red-brick Royal Bank and the old Hudson's Bay Company building, now occupied by Allison's Drug Store with its soda fountain counter and a post office. Mail is picked up here from a wall of locked, wooden slots painted a dark brown. Two women behind wickets are selling stamps and handle incoming and outgoing parcels.

A right turn from Carson Avenue takes us up Front Street, along the banks of the Fraser River. This is the main drag with the Cariboo and Quesnel hotels, with beer parlours that offer separate entrances for Ladies and Men; Fraser's General Store, Cowan's hardware, Hills Meat Market, and Allen's Bakery. On the next block up is the Rex Theatre. Owned by Mr. A.J. Elliot, this small theatre holds about a hundred people. It has both black leather seats, secured to the slanted floor, and some scattered wooden chairs. We don't go to shows very often because it costs money, but sometimes my sisters take me to a movie. It's exciting to enter the dimly lit room, to choose a chair and sit among so many strangers. *Snow White and the Seven Dwarfs* left me with nightmares. *Bambi* had me crying for days. At one movie, I was so terrified that I dove toward my sister and gave the chair in front of me with its occupant such a hard shove with my feet that both went flying down the room.

Leaving the theatre, you will find the telegraph office where telephone operators are working on a switchboard to put through telephone calls. There are only a few telephones around and if you have one, it is a party line. That means neighbours can listen to your private conversations. The street goes on past the hospital and joins roads to Wells, Barkerville, Prince George and points further north.

Turn right off Front Street onto Barlow Avenue, and you come to my father's store on the corner of Barlow Avenue and McLean Street. Pa-pah owns a block of Barlow Avenue—the store on one end and the house on the other. This area, known as Chinatown, isn't as busy as Front Street. There's the Nugget Café and Hotel, the Wah Lee building with herbal medicines, a corner store, laundries and a few private Chinese homes interspersed amongst them. Most of the Chinese here are bachelors, stranded on one side of the world with their families on the other.

That green and white clapboard house across the street from our house belongs to Granny Moffat. Notice her huge vegetable garden with chickens wandering around. Look at the raspberry bushes hanging over her picket fence. Sometime we warily snitch a few. "Get out of there, you kids," she shouts, and she stomps towards us. She has a fat body, puffy eyes, wispy grey hair and a very loud voice. We scramble back across the street, our cheeks full of berries. We know she is a kind person. When Ma-mah first came to Canada, Granny Moffat taught her how to knit and some of my sisters are named after her children.

Behind our house is the Public Works building. See that big grey building with a tower? Inside the tower hangs a massive bell attached to a rope, like the kind found in churches. This is the town's fire bell. It scares everyone when it rings in the dead of the night. We leap out of bed and rush to windows trying to spot the fire. The bell tolls a slow, eerie, deep droning sound—dong . . . dong . . . dong. The noise is scary and more so if you happen to hear a dog howl, because that means someone has died.

Graveyards, ghosts and dead people have always frightened me. Once my girlfriend, Sadie, suggested we cut across the graveyard to her house. She followed as I led the way. Suddenly she yelled, "Run, Lily, run!" She streaked past me and I followed at her heels. "Don't look back," she screamed. "One of the graves opened up and sand's flying in the air and there's a ghost chasing us." My hair stood up on end. We ran until we reached her bedroom and hid under the bed.

The Quesnel Bridge also leads to Dragon Lake, my favourite lake for swimming and skating. In summer we can walk the five kilometres to the lake. It is a hot and dusty grind up a steep hill with switchbacks. We sometimes use a shortcut trail, steep and rocky, that takes us to the top of the hill and back to the country road lined with alders. Sometimes a herd of fierce-looking cattle block the road and we take a wide detour to avoid them. We also avoid a haunted house because we have heard strange noises around it, and we have seen blue flickering lights nearby, a mystery we can't solve.

When we reach the lake, all sweaty and hot, we can light a bonfire, strip into bathing suits behind a clump of bushes, run out to the wharf and jump into the cold, sparkling waters. The walk home isn't as tiring because it is mostly downhill. One day, Walter Boyd, a customer at our store, said we kids could ride with him every Sunday to Dragon Lake in his open Ford car. What a windfall that was!

In winter we can skate on the whole surface of Dragon Lake before the snow falls. Do you know the tremendous feeling of freedom when skating on a frozen lake? Your adrenalin peaks as you soar across the ice swaying, turning, racing, and sniffing the fresh cold air brushing your face. Add to this ecstasy of your companions' exhilarated laughter and shouts of sheer enjoyment.

There is an outdoor skating rink in town, near the hospital, where we skate most of the time. It is a regular-sized rink enclosed by a wooden fence. After a blizzard, most everyone helps to shovel the snow off the ice. Soon the embankment of snow is as high as the fence. The ice surface is often a bit rough in spots, but it doesn't bother us. We just skate around the bumps and cracks. During a hockey game, we stand on the packed snowbank, bundled up like Arctic hunters, and shout for our team to win. If we are lucky, we will find a spot on the west side of the rink, under a shelter that has a couple of wood-fired heaters.

The second bridge that crosses the Quesnel River is the trestle of the Pacific Great Eastern railway. The railway line begins in Squamish, BC, and ends in Quesnel. My best friend, Patsy, and her sister and brother live on a farm across the river. They go to school in town and constantly use the railway trestle as a short cut.

Patsy runs across it like a deer in flight. I often walk to her farm on the trestle bridge, but it frightens me a little. The ties are set about six inches apart and I'm afraid of tripping if I don't watch my every step. The sight of the rushing river below makes me nervous. Sometimes when we are on the bridge we hear the train's whistle at the road crossing or feel its vibration on the rails as it approaches, blasting a warning whistle. When this happens, we jump off the tracks onto one of the cement footings, stand between wood structures and hang on for dear life. The bridge rocks as the heavy steam engine chugs slowly pass with its string of boxcars. I never tell my parents about these close encounters.

On the farm we just sit around together, or jump in the haystacks, or watch Patsy's mother milk cows or help her with the milk that she delivers daily around town. In the root cellar, a room dug into a side of a mound that smells like rotten potatoes, we gather turnips, potatoes and carrots to take into the house. I loved the sweet, pink honeysuckle bush that grows beside a garden patch.

The Fraser River Bridge is the longest of the three bridges. It connects Quesnel to West Quesnel. Built near the junction of the two rivers, it commands a beautiful view. From Front

Street you can look across the river to the west side, considered the seedy part of town. This neighbourhood isn't developed like the main village and the poor and transient people live here. However, this is not entirely true because some outstanding citizens reside here in some exceptional homes. You can see the impressive log house built by Mr. Marsh that houses his family of seven. There it is, on top of that hill overlooking the Fraser River and points beyond.

Can you see the hilly area we call Sugar Loaf? We hike its trails and feel like the King of the Castle when we reach the top. From that vantage point, we look below to the shanty houses of West Quesnel and count its outhouses.

Baker's Creek, the town's favourite swimming hole, is in West Quesnel. Its clear waters contain rapids, rocks and pools and drain into the Fraser River. Nearby, off the river, is a sandy bay called the Eddy. The boys built a diving board, which protrudes from the bank. This is where I learned to dive. Unfortunately, when we were children, a girl my age drowned and was washed down river. The Eddy was never used again.

Crossing the Fraser Bridge Pa-pah took us to the blueberry patch, to Six Mile Lake to fish and swim. My parents crossed it to enter the Nazko country where they hunted for moose and deer. A dirt and gravel road leads to the Nazko community and its cattle ranches. I remember watching a cattle drive cross the Fraser Bridge one fall. Cowboys in dusty, rain-stained hats yipped and yelled as they drove the cattle from the Nazko and Chilcotin areas into town. The noisy cattle thundered across the planked bridge towards the stockyards to be auctioned off.

One of the colourful characters from the Nazko area is a Hungarian trapper named Joe Spehar. He operates a store catering to the Nazko people. He is a grubby-looking old man with grey whiskers and a weather-beaten face. He wears a leather hat with ear flaps all year round, pulled down close to thick, scowling eyebrows. Despite his appearance, he is an amicable man who likes to chat the day away and toss back a jigger or two of whisky with my father. Every couple of months, before the snow flies, he drives into town in his Ford car to buy groceries, rolls of cloth, jeans, shirts and boots from our store to sell to his Nazko customers.

On Dominion Day, the Nazko families arrive in West Quesnel and set up camp with their families and horses. They've come to celebrate the holiday as well as to participate in the Quesnel rodeo. Many of these people crowd into Hoy's store and speak to Pa-pah in their Carriere language. The women have long braids, wear moccasins and western clothes. They buy cloth, tobacco and various sundries and offer in exchange beaded moccasins and gloves. We wander over to their camp to see the horses and my older sisters rent the horses for a dollar a day.

In school there is a boy in my class named Jim. I don't

know whether he comes from Nazko or where. He has big brown eyes, a shock of black hair, and a quiet disposition. He loves to chew Chiclets chewing gum. He laughs when we call him Chicaloo Jim. There are a couple of older boys like him in high school. I know of no other First Nations people living in town.

The Depression is ending in 1939, but I am so young that I am barely aware of the meaning of the Dirty Thirties. After the poverty of their upbringing in China, my parents are always so frugal. I assume we are poor, and have to make the best of what we have. Since we have a store we are never hungry. I remember once a man came to the back door and asked for food. I gave him some bread and butter.

In 2008, as I swing down the new highway to Quesnel, I notice that the shores of Dragon Lake are now lined with houses. The rodeo grounds house the Quesnel Museum and LeBourdais Park. A glass-structured town hall replaces the quaint, old Court House, and the main drag is now Reid Street rather than Front Street.

West Quesnel has mushroomed into a vicinity of its own with malls, restaurants, schools and modern amenities. A new second bridge for vehicles parallels the old one, which is now a footbridge.

Once a quiet farming town, Quesnel booms with sawmills and pulp mills that pollute the air. The village has become a city with paved streets, cement sidewalks, and impressive flower beds to beautify the town and impress tourists. An imposing walkway extends along the banks of the rivers.

Inevitably, Quesnel has changed since I was child. Without change, a community will die. The new city thrives on its new-found industries and multicultural society. But no matter how it changes, the old Quesnel will always be my hometown. My era is buried and forgotten by the younger generation, but my memories are there, fresh as buttercups in a field.

Chickens

I woke up with a start. I knew I had slept in. Oh, those poor chickens, cooped up in the old henhouse, I thought. I leapt out of bed, yanked off my pyjamas, slipped on a cotton dress, and stuck my feet into a pair of frayed runners.

I scurried downstairs, afraid if I didn't hurry, the chickens would die, if they weren't already dead. I tore out the kitchen door and through the garden gate into the backyard. The chicken house at the far end of the yard had once been a sturdy log cabin built in the early 1900s. It contained ten nesting boxes filled with straw, a three-tiered roost rack and a couple of dozen hens and a rooster.

The sun prickled the back of my neck. This was my first day of caring for the chickens while my parents were away. I had protested. "Why me? Why not Mooney? Why not someone else? I hate the smell of the chicken house, and I always get itchy when I go inside!"

"We all have chores to do around here," said Ma-mah. "You're ten years old and that's old enough take some responsibility."

"Okay, I'll do it, if I have to, but I don't want to."

The truth was, I really liked chickens. When we were little

kids we had watched Ma-mah mark a dozen eggs with a pencil and place them into a nest. She said that a hen would sit on the eggs until baby chicks were hatched. When that day came, we saw the chicks peer from under the mother hen. When Ma-mah retrieved a couple of chicks for us, the hen clucked nervously and pecked her hand. We cupped the yellow balls of fluff to our cheeks and twitched when their tiny claws pricked our hands. Later on, Pa-pah installed an incubator in the basement and we watched the chicks break through their shells.

My brothers and sisters often fed the chickens with garden greens, apple peelings and grains of wheat. We filled their water cans with a garden hose and playfully sprayed each other or the chickens just for the fun of it. Sometimes we hosed the rooster off the hens to stop him from hurting them.

Occasionally someone left the garden gate open and the chickens foraged through Ma-mah's vegetables. When this happened, she exclaimed, "Ayieh, ayieh! Who left the gate open?" She attacked the chickens with a corn broom and shouted, "Shoo, shoo, shoo." We joined the foray, jumped between the rows of vegetables, waved our arms, shouted and chased the frantic birds out the gate.

But the most fun was a game we called Chicken Hunting. When Ma-mah wanted a certain chicken for dinner she asked us to catch it for her. Using a long pole with a metal hook on the end, one of us squatted on her haunches amongst the flock and crept towards the designated victim. The chickens clucked and kept their distance, eyeing us suspiciously. But the stalker followed and when within hooking distance, quickly snagged the hen by its foot and dragged it squawking and flapping from the flock. One of us grabbed its feet and carried it to the house. We watched Pa-pah as he grasped its wings and head with one hand. With the other, he slit the chicken's neck with a long, sharp knife, gathering the blood into a container. He then tossed the bird on the ground. The hen flopped and jerked, spattering blood onto the grass.

When I was about six years old, I examined a hen soon after it was slaughtered. I crouched near the lifeless carcass and poked it with a stick while studying its closed eyes. Suddenly the bird flipped up, fluttered its wings and covered my face and clothes in blood. Frantically I stuck my head under a water tap, scrubbed my face, doused my hair and removed my stained, wet dress.

Ma-mah always cleaned the chickens in the kitchen sink. She poured boiling water over the feathers, plucked them, and then gutted the innards. The stink of wet feathers and gory guts sent us reeling out doors.

What I didn't like about chickens, now that I was older, was the stinky smell of the chicken house. Although the floor was swept and covered with fresh straw, the area under the roost remained heaped with chicken manure. Some of it was used for fertilizer, but most of it just sat in a solid lump.

When I reached the chicken house, I stood before the latched door. I heard the distressed chickens clucking and squawking as they strutted back and forth, back and forth, desperate to find an outlet. Through a grimy window they looked at me with yellow, beady eyes, their parched beaks agape and their Island Red feathers glistening.

The thought of opening the door in the summer heat and confronting a burst of half-crazed chickens made me shudder. I checked for a quick, unobstructed escape route. Tentatively, I unlatched the door hook, and then gently pushed the door slightly ajar. The pungent smell of frenzied chickens seeped through the opening. I held my breath and covered my nose and mouth with the collar of my dress. I gave the door a swift kick, and fled to the safety of the open yard. Frantic flying fowl burst like a feathered bomb behind me. Chickens scurried to the watering tins along the garden fence. They scooped water in their beaks and tilted back their heads, and their throats pulsated as they drank. The rooster, bearing beautiful plumage, strutted and crowed.

From a nearby shed, I scooped a tin of wheat kernels from a gunnysack. The wheat felt cool and slippery between my fingers. "Come little chickens, come, cluck, cluck, cluck," I beckoned. I threw a wide arc of kernels in the air and laughed to see them chicken-dance towards the feed. They pecked at the granules, rummaged for insects, cocked their red-comb heads and fluffed iridescent feathers. I noticed their different personality traits. Some followed, others led. Some stood alone, others socialized. Some sought shade from the sun, others burrowed in the ground to keep cool.

As I played with my feathered friends I was oblivious to the heat. I completely forgot about the muggy stench of the chicken house. Rose came running down the path from the store towards the house. "Hey, don't forget to collect the eggs!"

My chicken chore lasted ten years. It disappeared when the chickens, the chicken house, the garden and the backyard became the Hoy store's parking lot in the 1950s. Chickens still fascinate me. Whenever I see them range freely on local farms, I am reminded of my childhood. I think of how we learned as we experienced the life and death of chickens. Chicken houses and chicken yards are gone from my life, but not my love for chicken cacciatore, chicken potpie, chicken paprika. Ah, the list goes on.

As many as six Hoy sisters worked at the Hoy store at the same time. Here, Star and I laugh with some of the friendly staff who made our working day more fun.

Off to Work

My parents had a bunch of girls rather than a bunch of boys, so they treated us girls like boys—at least in the field of work. When there were chores to be done, everyone pitched in, whether it was helping in the store, running errands or doing housework. No job was considered too difficult for us to do. We were strong and healthy.

As the town grew in the 1940s, so did the business of Hoy's General Store. To keep up with its growth, Pa-pah ordered shipments of goods via freight train from the coast to Quesnel. When I was a young teenager, Pa-pah told us: "Come right home after school and help unload a shipment of flour."

We grimaced at the thought of the laborious task but learned never to complain or argue with Pa-pah. If you did, he stared at you over his spectacles in a way that left you feeling like a disobedient puppy.

After school, the girls changed into slacks and Benny into overalls. Rose, who worked in the store, joined us. We clambered onto the deck of our three-ton truck. Bert Foyle, the store's hired hand and long-time employee, grinned broadly at our sullen faces. "C'mon, girls, it's really not that bad." He drove us to the Pacific Great Eastern Railway station, and backed the truck to an open boxcar half-filled with hundred-pound sacks of Five Roses Flour.

We paired up and attacked the job. Grasping corner ends of the sacks, we hauled them onto the truck's deck and dropped them in a row. Giddiness overcame us as we trundled back and forth, lugging, heaving, and piling the sacks to fill the truck. We playfully nudged one another to get out of the way or staggered like drunks under the flour's weight. Bert cheered us on as he hoisted one sack after the other over his broad shoulders. Tomboy Rose, who carried her own load, especially amused him. We called her a show-off but she only laughed and said, "Aw, you guys are just lazy. There's nothing to it."

With the truck full, we climbed on top of the heap, flopped on our backs or sat to enjoy the fresh air. Our next job was to unload what we had just loaded.

At our flour warehouse, Bert backed the truck to the sliding door. We jumped from the truck onto a plank floor powdered with flour. Our voices echoed in the cavernous building, which smelled of dry, stale air. We convulsed with laughter at the sight of one another covered in flour-dust from head to foot.

"You look like a ghost. Boo!"

"You look like a white man!"

"You look like an old woman!"

Benny retrieved a steel wagon, and we loaded it with six or

seven sacks of flour. One of us pulled and steered, while others grunted and pushed the wagon to its designated spot. Again, we paired off and swung the sacks with a "one, two, three, heave" into a row. Soon the stack was higher than our heads. Benny, positioned on top of the stack, secured them. Even though we worked diligently, we also had fun. We accused each other of being slowpokes or clumsy-bums and yelled whenever a sack missed its target and tumbled to the floor. However, the fun stopped when Star screamed, "A mouse! A mouse! I saw a mouse!"

As if attacked by a grizzly bear, we shot out the door, leapt onto the truck or disappeared down the street—screaming, screaming. We blamed Bert for instilling the fear of mice into us. When we were kids, he had chased us with dead mice dangling between his fingers and threatened to stick them down our necks. Of course his threats were spoofs, but to this day, I believe I can still run faster than a mouse.

Every autumn, a woodsman delivered several cords of split, five-foot logs to the farthest corner of our backyard. He stacked them in rows of two, eight feet high and thirty feet long. With Ma-mah, we loaded the steel wagon, the one used to haul flour, and manoeuvred the cumbersome bulk over uneven terrain towards the house, and then shoved the logs down the basement chute. In the basement, two of us, amidst flying dust and chips, stacked the logs behind the furnace and between the furnace and the stairs. The poorly ventilated basement became a dust bowl that reeked of freshly cut wood.

In coldest winter, the chore of hauling wood to an uninsulated house seemed hopeless. Sometimes it snowed, sometimes the sun shone, but each time, our woollen mitts got soaked, our feet felt like blocks of ice, and our rosy cheeks stiffened.

Ma-mah swept the snow from the woodpile with a corn broom, and then axed the ice that cemented the logs together. We wiggled and pried apart the logs and then piled them onto our play toboggan. Ma-mah pulled and guided the toboggan slowly, while walking backwards. We pushed and struggled with the awkward load along the narrow path. The log ends sometimes scraped against the snow banks, causing the toboggan to slip sideways, almost toppling the wood. We chucked the logs down the chute, along with blasts of frigid air. Puddles of water accumulated on the cement floor near the woodpiles.

For years we burned wood in our kitchen stove. It was a cosy corner, our comfort zone. This cordial atmosphere ended when Pa-pah, in the late 1940s, replaced the wood stove with a sawdust burner. Then we began our Sawdust Experience. Where the sawdust came from I don't know, but apparently it was plentiful and cheaper to burn than wood. It was shipped in by boxcar and we had to unload it. "Here we go again," we groaned. "Where does Pa-pah get these weird ideas?"

Our friend, Bert Foyle,
a long-time worker
with C.D. Hoy & Co.

When Bert backed the truck into the boxcar's opening, we felt like the seven dwarfs in *Snow White*. "Hi ho, hi ho, it's off to work we go, with shovels in hand, to dig, dig, dig, a mountain of sawdust," we sang. The sawdust was light and dry as we scooped and tossed it from boxcar to truck. Clouds of dust plugged our noses. We sneezed and coughed; our hair turned orange and we itched all over.

When the truck was full, we sprawled on top for the ride home. Bert eased the truck to a woodshed with an opening near the roof. We shovelled the sawdust into the hole. When the pile inside got too high, two of us went into the shed, crawled up the mound and levelled the sawdust by sliding and pushing down with our feet and bums. At first it was fun to pretend it was a mountain of snow, but soon, we had sawdust up our pant legs, in our shoes, down our necks—and it felt like million ants were crawling over our skin.

The kitchen porch held four galvanized sawdust buckets, which had to be replenished with sawdust at least twice a day. Shoes tracked bits of sawdust into the house. No matter how carefully one dumped a bucket of the messy stuff into the stove's hopper, traces of sawdust layered the floor and stove.

In winter, the sawdust pile froze. We chipped the iceberg of sawdust with the shovel, whacked it and hauled the chunks to the house. But most frustrating was the sawdust hopper. Sometimes the sawdust stuck in the flue and had to be thumped to keep the fire burning. Other times, damp sawdust smouldered and filled the kitchen with smoke. Ma-mah called Pa-pah "a goddamn fool" for installing such a stupid stove in her kitchen. At last, an electric stove replaced the sawdust burner, and harmony resumed within our household. But neither the sawdust burner nor the electric stove could ever replace the wood burner with its beckoning warmth and Ma-Mah's never-empty teapot.

As I look back, I realize how our parents' work ethic trained us for the future and kept us out of trouble. Chores were taken for granted. They taught us challenges, responsibility, discipline, and kept us physically fit. It's unfortunate that many of today's children live their lives without chores, due partly to modern amenities and parents not insisting the chores be done. Kids spend time playing with expensive electronic toys, or they're driven from one sports activity to another. Yet I hear them say, "I'm bored." Chores too can be boring, but children who are given responsibility experience a sense of satisfaction and pride in giving back. I cannot compare my generation with today's generation. Life has changed so much—two working parents, guilt complexes, and affluence. But within these boundaries, I believe chores for children can only help them grow into strong, dependable adults.

Benny soaks up the sunshine on the shore of Dragon Lake, a favourite spot for summer swimming and winter skating. His life was cut short by a sudden, terrible illness.

Will God Punish Me?

My brother Benny and I were chums. We played with our siblings in our backyard: made mud-pies, splashed in an abandoned rowboat, sprinted in games of tag or roared up and down the sidewalk on a wagon.

When we started school together in 1937, our horizons broadened. The school playground replaced our backyard with games of softball and marbles; schoolmates joined our hikes, swims, skates and other activities. As teenagers, our paths gradually diverged. Benny turned towards Boy Scouts and male activities. His friend Mike told me about one of those activities. "We'd head down to Ernie Dawson's pool hall after school where there was a magazine rack and soft drinks, as well as the mystery of the pool tables further back in the room. Benny took great delight in showing us what could be found on the magazine rack between the covers of a journal called *Sunbathing* or some such thing. Pinup-girls they were not, but they were nude—not stylish, but inclined to overweight and perhaps a more realistic introduction to things forbidden than the other magazines available in those days."

Meanwhile, I joined my girl friends in Girl Guides.

Benny and our tomboy sister Rose, eight years his senior, became buddies. Rose was a gal full of energy and fun. Store customers admired her strength, spunk and friendliness. Like her, many of her friends were show-offs and daredevils. She almost drowned when someone dared her to swim across Ten Mile Lake. On Halloween they pushed over every outhouse they could find. We wondered if Rose had any common sense, but we knew she had a kind heart.

After our handyman Bert quit his job around 1945, Rose took over delivering groceries in the three-ton truck. Benny usually tagged along. One day I joined them on a rural delivery. When Rose turned off the highway towards the farm, Benny, who was fourteen said, "Let me drive." Rose, without thinking, agreed. Benny took the wheel, engaged the clutch and shifted the gears, and then stepped on the gas. The truck lurched forward, swayed wildly and careened down the winding road. I screamed and slumped to the floor. Rose yelled, "Stop! Stop! Stop!" Benny slammed on the brakes. The truck jolted to a stop, and the groceries went flying. "Jesus man, you trying to kill us!" Rose exploded. Thereafter, she taught him to drive properly. She also taught him how to handle a BB gun, how to spin a softball and how to dance. She became his confidante.

Benny was a good-looking boy with a thick mop of hair and rosy cheeks. He had a quiet disposition but we loved his company. Our parents loved and admired him, too, and taught him the responsibilities of a first son. He would carry the family surname, he would continue the family business, and he would care for them in their old age. However, Benny wasn't spoiled at the expense of the other children. Like the rest of us, he had chores, was taught about obedience, duty, hard work, moral character, and the value of money. He was neither showered with toys, offered special foods, nor given extra privileges nor undue attention. He did feel the subtle pressure of our parents' expectations. My younger brother Jack was spared this stress.

One Saturday afternoon as Benny helped Pa-pah open kegs of nails in the store, Dad began to talk to him. "Benny, you're lucky to be in school. I only had three years of schooling. I still can't read or spell very good, but I do my best. I come from a poor family. You work hard like me when I was your age. See what I have today—a good business, a big house, a car. Someday, this will all be yours. But you must work hard. I expect you to carry on with the store business, expand it and make good investments. Be a good citizen and be proud of your achievements."

Benny listened as he pried off the wooden cover from a keg, tossed the splintered wood into the stove. He shoved the keg of nails under the counter. "I'm not cut out to be a businessman," he said. "I don't have the brains. Jack's the brainy one. He's the one to take over the business, not me." But Pa-pah could only see his first son as heir to the family enterprise.

Benny brooded over his inadequacies. He never forgot he had failed the first grade, and it profoundly affected him. When we were kids, I didn't help matters. Whenever we had a disagreement, I flung his failure in his face to win an argument. He never retaliated. As he matured, his skills were in his hands. He could fix anything from broken bicycles to water pumps to electrical wiring. Rose urged Benny not to worry and to enjoy life while he was young

I remember when he turned fifteen, and wore his first suit—a bluish-grey tweed. He stood five foot nine, slim and boyish. "Hubba, hubba, ding ding," I said. He blushed and ran his fingers through his mop of black hair.

Shortly after, he complained of a sore upper left arm. He said he couldn't remember having hurt it.

"Maybe you fell on one of your Scout hikes," I said.

"I don't think so," he said. "I would have remembered."

The throbbing pain lingered, and Ma-mah slathered Sloan's Liniment onto the affected area. Later Dr. Baker diagnosed it as a muscle injury and taped the arm against his body. That night Benny suffered excruciating pain. "Jesus Christ, Jesus Christ," he cried and ripped off the bandages and flung them on the floor.

A biopsy revealed the culprit was cancer. Cancer? Somewhere we'd heard about the disease, but didn't know anyone who had it. What was it? What did it mean? It was a word that wasn't even in our vocabulary. We aimlessly searched for answers. No one really knew what it was except that it was a killer disease. We were terrified.

Doctors knew little about treating cancer in the 1940s. Dr. Baker suggested the possibility of amputation, which terrified Benny. He begged not to have his arm cut off.

"No, Benny, they won't do that," I said. "They're only talking. Everything is going to be all right, you'll see." At the same time I worried because I knew his hands were his lifelines.

The arm wasn't amputated, but there was nothing the doctors could do. They recommended a visit to the Mayo Clinic, the foremost cancer research institution in Minneapolis, Minnesota. On a dull October day, Dad, Benny and Rose flew to Minneapolis. After a week of tests at the Mayo Clinic, the results were positive and the doctors advised that Benny return home and be made as comfortable as possible.

At home, Ma-mah nursed Benny, but the cancer grew and the pain intensified as he continued to cry out. We suffered with his anguish but could do little to comfort him. An ambulance took him to the hospital where a nurse injected him with morphine. Ma-mah stayed with Benny. She wrapped his arm in a poultice of pungent Chinese herbs; she mixed a concoction of herbs for him to drink. She prayed for him to live.

Benny languished, pale and thin with a cold sore on the right side of his mouth. By now he had accepted the inevitable. Even Pa-pah's promise of a new car, upon getting well, didn't matter. Rose slept in a cot near him and one day he turned his sad, brown eyes to her and said, "What's it like in Heaven?"

"Everything will be well," she said. "Your arm will heal and you'll be free of pain. And don't be afraid because very soon, we'll all be together again."

Benny's swollen arm felt and looked like yellow parchment. Extra doses of morphine no longer helped. In anguish he continued to cry out, "Jesus Christ! Jesus Christ!" then pathetically asked, "Will God punish me for swearing?"

One day as Ma-mah and Rose watched over him, a stream of blood abruptly shot from his arm like an arched arrow. Rose caught it in a bedpan as Benny whispered, "Doctor," and closed his eyes. Rose reached for his hand. Ma-mah stopped her, as she superstitiously said, "No, don't touch him, or death will try to take you too."

Suddenly the door opened. Rose went to close it but it wouldn't close. They knew he had gone.

Five months after his cancer diagnosis, Benny died on March 5, 1947, nineteen days before his sixteenth birthday.

It was snowing as mourners gathered at St. Andrews United Church. After the service, following Chinese custom, the funeral cortege drove through Chinatown, and then past our house, before going to the cemetery. Large flakes of snow fell gently as Benny's coffin was lowered with his Scout hat on top. Our village mourned the death of a boy whose birth had brought jubilation.

First son.

One hundred days of mourning followed Benny's death. During this time we abstained from participating in any social functions. Although we routinely attended school or went to work, we kept much of our feelings to ourselves. We knew Rose agonized over Benny's death, thinking she could have done more to save him. For a while she withdrew within herself, angry at the world, angry with us, because she felt we didn't care, yet she said nothing.

Benny's death devastated Ma-mah and Pa-pah. In the first week they refused to leave their bedroom. They blamed themselves for his death and then, they blamed him. "He's not our son. Our son wouldn't do this to us. He wouldn't leave us." Uncle Joe, Pa-pah's brother, brought them to their senses and made them realize that they had responsibilities and other children.

Pa-pah buried his grief in his work. His store and his customers became his saviours. He never spoke to us about Benny. Once, after twenty-three years, he showed me a picture of Benny in his wallet and said, "Do you remember him?"

Ma-mah never got over Benny's death. She became afflicted with psoriasis, a skin disease that marked her face and body. She seldom spoke of Benny, but we knew he was always on her mind. She spent many evenings in the basement after his death, seated before the open furnace, stoking the fire, singing softly, tears running down her face. Here was her sanctuary, where she could be alone with her thoughts, alone with her first son.

Jack inherited Benny's place in the family. He knew his position in the family hierarchy and stepped into it unobtrusively after high school.

Jack accepted new responsibilities in the Hoy family as the only remaining son in the family business after Benny's death.

Tale of a Fisherman

"Hush, hush, it's all right, it's all right," Ma-mah cooed as she rubbed Jackie's little hands with ointment. She held him firmly but gently. Jackie screamed and wiggled to be free. She held on as she bandaged his hands covered in eczema with a roll of gauze. Over these bandages she tied on white cotton mitts to prevent him from pulling off the bandages and scratching his hands until they bled. "There, there, it's all finished," she said, releasing her hold on him. He slipped from her lap and pulled at the mitts, rubbed his hands together and cried. This scene was repeated many times until he was about three or four years old.

Jack, my youngest brother, the eleventh child, was born sickly. I remember that he cried a lot. Ma-mah and my older sisters carried and comforted him. Although Jack was part of my early childhood, I don't remember him as vividly as the others. His illness often stopped him from playing with us, but when he was well, he joined in with gusto. Sometimes he stopped to catch his breath; sometimes he defied the odds and suffered the consequences. He was a fighter and never gave up. Around the age of four, his eczema cleared enough to dispense with bandages. Despite poor health, he was a chubby little guy with big brown eyes and an easy laugh.

Our parents encouraged us to be independent, and their attitude to Jack was no exception. He was pampered, but not spoiled. He had chores to do and understood the household rules of obedience, humility and respect. My parents knew Jack was intelligent and quick-witted. They watched over him but gave him enough freedom so that he could discover his own capabilities. Unfortunately, Jack would be plagued with eczema, asthma and food allergies for the rest of his life.

In school he was a quiet lad with a glint of mischief in his eye who somehow brought home good report cards. He played a wicked game of marbles with his schoolmates but was unable to participate in basketball or softball. These sports winded him and irritated his hands. He turned to what he liked best— fishing.

As a wee tyke, he fished with Ma-mah and Pa-pah even when he wasn't feeling well. He was the first in the boat and the last out. Pa-pah taught him the skills of trolling and fly-fishing. They practiced casting a rod and reel in the backyard at the expense of the squawking chickens. Later, Pa-pah also taught him how to hunt for wild game and birds.

Jack had a good sense of humour. One Christmas, when he was about twelve, he gave each of the girls a little present, beautifully wrapped in shiny red paper and tied with white satin ribbon. We marvelled at his creative ability and carefully opened the gift. To our surprise we each found a stick of Juicy Fruit chewing gum. "A stick of gum!" We collapsed in laughter. "Not even a package, but a stick! How cheap can you get?" Jack enjoyed our reaction and said, "You're too many sisters, and you're lucky I didn't give you a half a stick." And Irene flicked him with the tea towel he gave her. She hated doing dishes and he knew it.

One time he cycled out to Dragon Lake to go swimming. On his way back down the steep, switchback road, he missed a turn, hit the rocky embankment and flew into a clump of bushes. At home, I found him flat in bed, his face a mess. He had dabbed Mercurochrome, a red disinfectant onto his scratches with swabs of cotton batten.

Tufts of cotton stuck to his face like upside-down tutus on a field of red. "My God," I said, "Are you okay? What happened? You look like you belong in a Frankenstein movie." He opened a puffy eye and said, "That bad, eh?"

"Yeah, that bad." I gently washed his face and plucked off the cotton tufts as he yelped. "How'd you get home?"

"Walked."

"Where's the bike?"

"In the bush."

"You do look like a clown."

"I feel like the guy on the flying trapeze who missed the net."

As a young kid, and later as we grew up, I always thought

I had Jack under my wing when we swam, skated or partied together. How wrong I was. In time I realized I depended more on him than he did on me. And what a trooper he was to come to my aid when I needed him.

When I was seventeen, and in Grade Eleven, I used Jack as a decoy when I had a crush on the new schoolteacher. Oh, how we high school girls giggled and swooned when twenty-year-old Bertin Webster, six foot three, blond and blue-eyed, strode past us and entered his elementary classroom. He was also our Physical Education teacher. We gave him two thumbs up.

As fate would have it, not only was this handsome young man Jack's Grade Eight teacher, but he also took an interest in me. In time he asked me to a movie. I refused. It was a no-no for Hoy girls to date white boys, but I liked this man. One day I invited him over to the house because he wanted to meet my parents. I was nervous and flustered.

"Jack, you've got to help me," I implored my younger brother. "You've got to promise me that you'll be home when he comes, or I'll die!"

"Okay, but it'll cost you," Jack replied.

When our guest arrived, I told my parents that Mr. Webster was Jack's teacher and that he had come to see them. My parents had great respect for teachers and greeted him warmly. And so it was that we casually dated, while the town gossiped, perhaps with my parents' misgivings. Bertin would become my first husband; we married twelve years after that first visit.

I also depended on Jack to take me duck hunting with his buddies in the Chilcotin area. I tagged along to admire the scenery, to enjoy the fresh air and their company. One day Jack said, "Okay, sis, if you come with us, you carry a gun." I purchased a ten-gauge shotgun and he taught me how to trap shoot. One frigid morning somewhere in the Chilcotin, the group of us squatted, hidden in the bulrushes beside a lake. We waited and waited. "Ssh, don't talk or move or the ducks won't come," Jack whispered. Suddenly a flock of ducks flew overhead. "Shoot!" I pointed my gun and fired, but by then, the ducks were gone. To my surprise, they returned. "Shoot!" I stood and gaped as the flock winged pass. That ended my career as a duck hunter.

Although Jack enjoyed hunting, his passion was fishing. He took me out a few times in a rowboat, but serious fishing was reserved for friends like Ron Mattison and a couple of other buddies. They seized every opportunity to fish. They followed the fish in season: salmon, steelhead, rainbow trout or the feisty Dolly Varden. They drove over rugged logging roads spiked with rocks and boulders; they hiked trails strewn with fallen logs and overgrowth; they flew into remote bays and inlets—to reach rivers, lakes and oceans where the fish were biting. They went in rain and wind, snow and sleet, sunshine and showers and they usually caught more fish than they could eat. They fished in the misty dawn; they fished by moonlight and they ice-fished on frozen lakes. And each trip had a story of its own. Ron told me this one:

"Once when we fished the Dean River, we spotted a grizzly bear enter the river from the opposite side and swim towards us. Not wanting to fool around with a grizzly, we grabbed our fishing gear and hightailed it up the bank, ran into the woods and along a trail towards the safety of our vehicle. Jack huffed and puffed and wheezed to keep up. When we stopped for him to take a whiff of his puffer, he looked behind him and said, 'Geez, I sure hope that bear don't like Chinese food.' That cracked us up and we sat and rested with a wary eye peering down the trail."

I admired Jack's stamina and fortitude. He carried a heavy burden. When our brother Benny died, Jack was only thirteen. He knew the responsibility of the Hoy business would rest on his shoulders. How he felt as a child or as an adult, to be Second Son, I don't know. We never talked about it. Perhaps he was happy that Pa-pah did not exert the same pressure on him that Benny had known. Maybe he just accepted his role in the scheme of things. I don't know. His health was a deep concern throughout his life, and he had to contend with ten bossy sisters.

What sustained this remarkable person? Intelligence and a zest for living, I think. Jack was strong-willed and faced adversity without complaint. His winsome personality coupled with his sense of humour attracted good friends, such as Ron Mattison.

Their friendship was built on trust, respect and fishing. Through the darkest hours of Jack's life, Ron was there. When Jack was critically ill with cancer, the fish beckoned, and Ron took him to their favourite fishing hole.

Above all else, Jack had the good fortune to marry a fine woman in 1960. Geraldine came from a Manitoba family of ten girls and two boys and fitted right into our family. Gerri understood Jack's predicament and stood stoically beside him with patience and understanding. She worked in the store and dutifully helped to care for our aging parents. As well, she encouraged him to use his creative talents to paint in oils and to photograph nature. Their friends were many; they had a good and loving relationship, raised two sons—and she also fished.

Jack managed the Hoy business with our brother-in-law, Martyn Lore, Anne's husband, to a successful end. The store sold in 1979. Jack then managed the sports department in Willis Harper Hardware before his retirement. On the day Jack retired, he relaxed on his garden patio soaking up the sun. His neighbour, Phyllis, from across the street yelled, "Hey, Hoy, why ain't cha working?" Without a pause, he replied: "My wife works, my car works, why should I work?" Jack's life was short, but he lived it fully and actively. He died at the age of fifty-four, a happy man.

On the Legion's front steps before a dance rehearsal, I showed off my costume along with Connie Murray, Lil Marsh, Joy Hobbins, my sister Mooney and Sharon Bryden.

The Magical Legion Hall

I open a letter from my friend, Jean. "Did you know the Legion Hall burnt down?" Oh, no. My thoughts whirled back to my childhood, to my teenage and adult years within its four walls. I remembered the old wooden structure, not particularly handsome but embracing us in its solid simplicity. It had been my home away from home, my magical kingdom.

The magic started in 1937 when I performed in my first Christmas concert in the Legion. My teacher, Helen Ferguson, prepared her classes for the event. We practiced our song and dance routine to a portable, windup gramophone while Miss Ferguson counted and clapped "one, two, three, kick, and turn," over and over again. After classes, we trudged the snow path to the Legion for dress rehearsal. Once inside, we stomped our snowy feet in the foyer before entering the main hall. We discarded our coats, hats and mittens and heaped them onto wooden benches and chairs before taking our seats, waiting for our turn.

Evergreen branches with red bows graced the front edge of the theatre. A tall Christmas tree glittered silver and gold under coloured lights, and costumed performers moved through the shadowed hall to the stage. I sat mesmerized by the unfamiliar, fantastical scene before me. When our turn came, we giggled and stumbled through our dance routine to the pounding of an upright piano. Tomorrow was the great performance before our parents. I knew sleep wouldn't come that night.

The Legion Hall became our school gymnasium throughout my junior and senior years. Twice a week we tumbled and exercised to earn school credits. After school, we spent hours playing basketball and badminton or watching annual sports competitions with visiting teams from Wells, Prince George and Williams Lake.

The Legion Hall was not just a place for sports. Lured on by my favourite teacher—Miss Ferguson had become Mrs. Dixon by then—I participated in her high school dramas and her dance group. We performed plays and folk dances for various Legion socials. Practices, rehearsals and adjudicated performances—all make-believe—happened in the Legion. We launched Teen Town in 1946. I became its Mayor in 1947. The Legion offered its Annex as our headquarters for meetings and social events, and never charged us for the use of the building. Every Friday night we reeled, jived and waltzed to long-play 33⅓ RPM records in a gathering of good friends. No one drank or smoked. It was a different time.

After my school years, Saturday dances at the Legion became the highlight of the week. When our store locked its doors at

Our basketball team, The Hot Shots, sometimes had five Hoy sisters playing. We confused our opponents because we all looked alike, especially in our uniforms.

nine, the Hoy sisters rushed through the routine of closing up—
sweeping the floor, covering the counters with cotton sheets,
cashing up—and then dashed home to change into dressy attire.
Our dates picked us up or we went with a group of friends. By
the time we arrived, the joint rocked as dancers jived, galloped
the schottische, twirled the polka or waltzed sentimentally to
the music of Bob Hendry or The Devil Dreamers. At one AM
the orchestra swung into the Home Waltz.

"What's a Home Waltz?" my daughter asked, years later.

Surprised at her ignorance, I explained the Legion ritual.
"It's the last dance of the evening. It's when you snuggle up to
your partner, cheek to cheek, and dreamily waltz to 'Good Night
Sweetheart,' 'A West, a Nest and You,' 'The Tennessee Waltz,' and
other golden goodies."

"Cool," she said.

We needed special skills to decorate that plain, old Legion
for special events such as Halloween, Burns Night, Valentine's
Day and Christmas. No matter how hard we tried to beautify its
walls, or adorn tables with tablecloths and flowers, a romantic
ambience was impossible—unless the lights went out. From
1937 until I left Quesnel in 1958, I remember good times at
the Legion. It was a place in a small community where people
could gather, share ideas, and nurture lifelong friendships.

I have a trophy that commemorates one event in the Legion.
The trophy belonged to the Hot Shots, a basketball team

sponsored by Hoy's store. The team included four Hoy sisters: Rose, Yvonne, Star and me. We sisters played forward while the taller girls, Lillian Marsh, Lily Thompson, Faye Hodges and Ruth Love, generally played guards. Our forward winning strategy, because we were short, was a fast bounce-past game. The Hoy girls also took advantage of the fact that we looked alike, especially in uniform, which confused our opposition.

That tarnished silver trophy represents a winner—the Legion Hall, my magical haunt. The year after the fire, a modern Legion Hall was built to accommodate the community's needs with a lounge, a sports bar, and a smaller hall. There wasn't anything left of the old hall except a sign, "Legion Branch No. 94," and the memories that no fire could destroy.

Looking forward to a bright future, my sister Irene posed in her high school graduation gown in 1955. She died just two years later, and took a secret with her.

My Sister Irene

Irene was the baby of our family. Because she was so much younger than her sisters, she was somewhat neglected. Even Ma-mah didn't have much time for her. Of all the sisters, I was the nearest in age, but a seven-year gap doesn't make for a close relationship. We did spend time together. We swam and skated on the local lakes, talked about boys, and occasionally partied with mutual friends. In the summer of 1954, when she was seventeen and I was twenty-four, we shared a holiday on the beaches of California.

After graduating from high school in 1955, Irene worked in our father's general store for a year. She was a pretty girl with a round face, fair complexion, flirty eyes and a generous smile. That smile and flirtatious look aroused in Jim Dickson, a branch manager of a small distributing company, a consuming, passionate love from which he never recovered. However, Irene wanted something more than store work, something more than what Quesnel could offer. She moved to Vancouver to take a business course.

A year later, on a July afternoon, I returned home from a three-day hike up in the Cariboo Mountains. I swung open the kitchen door and yelled, "Hi, Ma-mah. I'm back, tired, and hungry!"

"Oh, Lily-ah, I wish you had come earlier," said Ma-mah, as she towelled her hands. "Irene was home. She left a couple of hours ago for Vancouver. Said she had to work tomorrow."

"Oh, darn her! Why didn't she tell us she was coming? I would have stayed home and waited for her." I dropped my backpack on the floor and rushed upstairs to my bedroom, hoping she'd left me a note. We hadn't seen each other for more than a year, and I missed her.

I stepped into my bedroom, the room that was hers until she went away. It looked the same as when I left it three days earlier. The two double beds, separated by an antique dresser, remained neatly covered with white chenille bedspreads with faded flower designs. I knew she wasn't here, but I felt her presence. A freakish feeling, a ghostly sensation, gripped me.

I felt myself drawn slowly into the room. I glanced around in search of a note. Nothing. I noticed the indentation of someone having sat on the bed. It wasn't an impression of a body sprawling out comfortably and relaxed. No. The body had been perched briefly. I looked at the cigarette in the ashtray on the dresser. There were no ashes. She'd taken maybe a puff or two, then with a deliberate twist, left a broken, filtered cigarette. Unconsciously, she had left a message. I knew she was troubled.

Three months later, Irene was buried at Forest Lawn Cemetery in Burnaby. The oxygen tent hadn't saved her, neither could our two nursing sisters. The Asian flu had consumed her. She died at the age of twenty, on October 27, 1957.

Friends and relatives gathered at the graveside. Next to me stood her boyfriend Jim, tall, thin and handsome. I glanced at his drawn, pale face as he bit his lower lip. "He's really suffering," I thought, and then realized it was more than that—he looked tormented. I slipped my hand into his.

"Thanks," he said.

After the service, Jim and I walked slowly to the reception hall. He was deep in thought. Finally, he turned to me and quietly said, "Did you know Irene had a baby girl?"

"What?" I stopped in my tracks. "No, I didn't know. Please, tell me about it."

"She had the baby four months ago. We put her up for adoption. A Scottish couple adopted her. None of your family knew. She definitely didn't want your mom and dad to know. It would have disgraced them, and they would've disowned her. Even though we loved each other, she wouldn't marry me."

The next day, before heading back to Quesnel, my brother Jack and I stopped by her grave. A cascading mound of flowers covered it. "Good-bye, Irene," I said. I plucked a white rose from a wreath, and set it gently on the inside of the car's rear window.

We reached home that evening and parked the car behind our house. Family and friends greeted us with food and comfort. As we relaxed amid the hubbub of chatter, I suddenly remembered the rose. "Oh," I said, "I forgot to bring in the flower I took from Irene's grave."

I ran out into the dark, autumn night. The lights from the kitchen windows shone down the path towards the car. As I opened the back door, I saw the rose, fresh and bright as it had been upon her grave. A glint of light touched its petals and it seemed to glow. As I reached for it, my arm froze in mid-air as if paralyzed. Superstitious thoughts of death, imbedded since childhood from my Chinese heritage, surged through my mind—don't touch death, or it will take you too. Don't bring death into the house, it's bad luck. I forced myself to seize the flower, and then fled to the house.

Back in the cheery kitchen, I tried to dismiss the experience. I dropped the rose into a crystal glass and placed it on the table. Soon after, the guests left. My girlfriend, Jean stayed with me.

Up in the bedroom, I placed the rose on the dresser. We crawled into our beds. No sooner had I snuggled down when my body began to shake and I broke into a cold sweat. I felt the flower's presence: haunting and ethereal, watching me, enveloping me.

"Jean! Jean!" I cried out. She sprang out of bed.

"What is it? What's the matter?"

"Get that flower out of here," I gasped.

She took the rose from the room. After that I could sleep.

Forty-five years passed. I had neither seen Jim, nor heard about him. I had often thought about their child, my niece, and wondered if I should try to contact her. In April 2002 I began writing my memoirs and started a file on Irene. Among the gathered photos is a snapshot of Irene and Jim. They are cuddled together on a chesterfield. His left arm embraces her shoulder, and he appears to be whispering into her ear. Irene glows as she smiles into the camera, her left leg tucked under her, her head on his shoulder.

One evening, I was at home in Courtenay when the telephone rang.

"Lily, is that you?" It was my sister-in-law, Gerri.

"Yeah, it's me, what's up?"

"You won't believe it! You won't believe what I'm going to tell you!"

"Tell me, tell me, what is it?"

"Last week a guy phoned and asked for Irene. He wanted to contact her for some sort of a reunion. When I said she had passed away, he apologized and hung up. Now, just a few minutes ago, the same guy called back. He said his name was Mike Dunn. He is married to Kathy—Irene's daughter."

"You're kidding!"

"No, no, I'm not! I told him I'd have you call him this evening."

I immediately called my sister Star in Victoria. She was

delighted to hear about Kathy, a new niece. "You know," she said, "Jim phoned me last year. I was sick in bed so Max talked to him. He left his phone number, but I haven't been able to reach him. Perhaps you can. And by the way, he has never married."

When I called the Dunns, both Kathy and Mike were as eager to meet me as I was to meet them. We planned a get-together the following week in Burnaby. I invited my chatty and vivacious niece, Linda, to accompany me. I felt Kathy should meet a relative closer to her own age, and I knew they would love her. Next I contacted Jim in Vancouver. I told him who was calling and for a moment, there was a pause.

"Lily? Irene's sister?"

We talked of old times, but he kept referring to Irene. He talked again of his love for her. I suggested we meet for coffee the next time I was in Burnaby. I wanted to see what he was like after so many years. I never mentioned that I was in contact with his daughter.

On April 7, 2002, Linda and I welcomed Kathy and Mike into our family. Linda threw open her arms and encircled them with big hugs. Her burst of energy sparked an eruption of laughter with everyone talking at once. Kathy and Mike presented me with a copper container filled with various types of plants. She had once worked for a greenhouse company, but now kept books for her husband's trucking firm.

I looked for Irene's resemblance in Kathy. Yes—the expressive brown eyes, fair skin and engaging smile belonged to Irene. Apart from that, she had her own Eurasian beauty: oval face, straight nose, high cheekbones and black, shoulder-length hair.

Mike's rugged face beamed. He had instigated the search for Kathy's birth mother. He felt she should know her roots even though Kathy had never had the urge to find Irene. She was happily married with two children, Michael and Jenny, and her adoptive mother, Ethel, lived close by. She had feared the unknown. They studied the photos of Irene and Jim, and looked for similarities between the parents, Kathy, and the kids. At one point Mike exclaimed, "Michael looks just like his grandfather. No wonder the kid doesn't look like me!"

I observed them closely as lunch extended into supper. They appeared relaxed and happy, and spoke freely on various issues, including Irene and Jim. Assured that everything was under control, and Kathy quite secure about her past, I said, "Would you like to meet Jim?"

With a startled look, Kathy clasped her hands to her chest. "Oh yes, I want to know everything." I said I had spoken to Jim briefly on the phone, but that I knew little about him and hadn't seen him since Irene died. We agreed to meet the following week, on April 15.

The next day I phoned Jim and invited him to join Linda and I for supper. The man who answered the door was an older version of the man I remembered. He stood tall and slender.

Wavy, silver hair replaced his 1950s crewcut, and dark-rimmed glasses framed his brown eyes. He wore polished shoes, black slacks and a tailored shirt.

"Come in and see my digs," he said.

His bachelor flat was clean, neat, and simply furnished. A double bed in a corner, a chest of drawers, a kitchen table with four chairs, an easy chair, a television, a fridge and stove. On the chest of drawers stood a framed, black-and-white photo of Irene in her graduation gown.

"Well, what do you think of my palace?" he asked. "I just had the rug cleaned, and I painted the table and chairs last week. I must've known you were coming." He spoke with a Scottish accent.

Shortly after Irene died, Jim had purchased a one-way ticket back to Scotland. He missed Canada and central heating and returned within two weeks.

"I worked for three printing supply companies. The last one closed when I was sixty-one, then I couldn't find another job. I hassled Superstore to hire me as a greeter. That lasted until I was sixty-four, when my knees gave out. I sold my car and now take public transportation."

While relating his work history, he continuously referred to Irene and his love for her, but failed to mention his daughter.

"Have you ever tried to find your daughter?" I asked.

He sighed, and nodded. "Oh yes, I've looked for years.

I've returned to the adoption agency time and again. They said a Scottish couple adopted her and that her name was Kathy Stewart. I once saw a wedding announcement for a Kathy Stewart in a Surrey newspaper. My buddy and I checked it out, but it wasn't her. I've never been able to locate her."

"Do you want to find her?"

"She's my daughter. I want to know if she's happy. I've never stopped loving her or her mother. I'd be the happiest guy in the world if I found her."

"Would you like to meet her?" I asked. "We were with her and her husband yesterday. She wants to meet you."

Jim almost staggered as he rose from his chair. "I think I need a beer."

On the appointed day, my husband, Frank, picked Jim up before the Dunns' arrival. "What will I say? How should I act? Will she like me? Will she accept me?" Jim shifted on the chesterfield and lighted one cigarette after the other out in the patio. When the doorbell rang, he followed me to the door. Father and daughter eyed each other timidly, embraced, and exchanged greetings. Jim presented Kathy with a bouquet of flowers. Mike introduced himself.

"Make yourselves comfortable while we prepare lunch," I said.

To ease the formality between them, Frank and I strolled

into the front parlour with a birthday cake and sang, "Happy Birthday to you, Jim." It was his sixty-ninth birthday. Everyone joined in, and broke the ice. Kathy and Jim chatted easily, shared cigarettes and got to know each other. Before departing, Jim suggested a planned visit to Irene's grave.

Unfortunately, I wasn't able to go with them to visit Irene's grave. Mike drove Kathy, Jim and Ethel to Forest Lawn Cemetery on a June afternoon. Afterwards, Ethel described the event to me.

She said that Jim thought he knew approximately where Irene's gravesite was because he used to go there frequently. However, they had difficulty finding it and wandered over the sprawling grounds beneath an umbrella. Ominous clouds hung dark and heavy in a bleak, grey sky and the rains came. Despite wet feet they persisted.

Ethel said, "From the comfort of our car, Mike and I watched the two—father and daughter—one seeking for her mother, the other, for his lover. We watched as they discovered her headstone. We watched as they bent down, their heads together, to read the inscription on the copper plate. We watched as they placed yellow roses on her grave. Suddenly, the rain stopped. Threatening clouds rolled back like a curtain on a stage. Sunlight streaked down from a blue sky. We saw them turn, look skyward, then at each other."

As I listened, a shiver went up my spine. Tears wet my cheeks. I knew Irene was finally at peace. She had spoken to me in my bedroom, before I knew she had a child; she had spoken to me from her grave, after I knew she had a child.

Her message to me had been clear: find my child, watch over her, and tell her my story.

Jim and Kathy retain a friendly relationship. They keep in touch by telephone—the Dunns live in Langley, in the Fraser Valley, and Jim lives in Vancouver. They get together on special occasions: birthdays, Father's Day, Christmas and the occasional visit to the horse races at the Exhibition Grounds in Vancouver. On August 9, 2007, Jim became a great-grandfather to Madisyn, his grandson's daughter. He knew the moment he held her that Irene was with him, ever caring, ever watching, as their family continues to grow.

The desk holds many secrets, many stories.

The Desk

"Come in, come in!" Ursula welcomed me into her home in Lake Cowichan, on Vancouver Island. I followed her as she balanced precariously between two walking canes to a chesterfield covered by a bright, crocheted afghan. She wore tailored slacks and a floral blouse that hung loosely from her thin body. Her sparkling green eyes enlivened a slender, wrinkled face. We hadn't seen each other in forty-three years.

Ursula had a strong voice despite her eighty-nine years. We spoke about current events, political turmoil and the World Series, but our conversation centred mainly on our past and present lives, and on those people whom we both knew, dead and alive, who had lived in Quesnel.

"That desk, over there, belonged to your Dad." Ursula pointed towards the far corner of the room, past her collection of antique chairs, stools, lamps and books.

I rose from my seat to take a closer look at the secretary desk and bookcase. A kerosene lamp, half-filled with yellow liquid and affixed with a glass chimney, sat on the top shelf. The open desktop revealed writing essentials neatly slotted and books lined the open shelves. I pushed aside a couple of old newspapers and gently ran my hand over the polished oak surface. I remembered the desk as part of my father's office furniture.

As children during the 1930s, my brothers and sisters and I would wander over to the store to amuse ourselves in Pa-pah's office while he worked in the hardware department. We would punch the adding machine keys and yank the handle until the paper tape reached the floor. We fingered the Underwood typewriter with its black and red ribbon and scribbled on sheets of paper. This desk stood between Pa-pah's large one and a small, white table with a drawer. Back then, it was barely discernible under dusty sheaves of outdated invoices, letterhead marked with the store's establishment in 1913, leather-bound ledgers, tattered receipt books and a box of white paper curled at the edges.

Throughout my childhood and teenage years the old desk was a junk collector in a small office with barred windows and makeshift furniture. And when in the 1950s, it disappeared amid the expansion of the store, I never noticed its absence, nor did I miss it. Seeing it again in my friend's house aroused my curiosity and a need to connect with its history.

"Where did it come from? How did you get it?"

"From your Dad," she said. "When I managed Hoy's dry goods department, back in the 1960s, I found it upstairs in the old section of the store. It was pushed against the log walls, hidden behind a stack of packing boxes. He sold it to me for five dollars."

Seeing the polished desk filled me with longing, and I knew I had to have it. "Ursula, if you ever decide to sell it, would you please, give me first refusal?"

She contemplated for a moment, then smiled and murmured in her English accent, "Well, well, now wouldn't that be interesting? That it should go back from whence it came."

Three years later, Ursula died. She left Pa-pah's desk to me in her will.

The desk is now part of my bedroom furniture. It is the first thing I see in the morning and the last thing at night. It draws my attention, and I often wonder how such a simple piece of furniture, without intricate scrolls and motifs, can be so intriguing. Perhaps its simplicity attracts me. It is as plain and simple as the pioneer days when it was built. The five neatly fitted shelves hold some of my favourite books—John Steinbeck, Margaret Laurence, Alice Munro. The drop-leaf cover, embellished with a rectangular row of wooden knobs, conceals my collection of journals, letters, pens and pencils.

Why does this desk captivate me? Is it because it belonged to my father? Is it because it was part of my own history? Is it because of what Ursula said?

"Look here," she had said the day she showed me the desk. She peered beneath a shelf and pointed at two charred spots.

"Your Dad said he used to work with a kerosene lamp on this desk, and over the years, the heat from the flames left indelible marks."

I gently rubbed the rough spots with my fingers. The touch conjured up a picture of Pa-pah as a young immigrant seated at the desk wearing a cheap black suit, brushing a letter home to China. His silhouette gleamed in the dim light of the flickering lamp. The imagery startled me and I realized the desk had told me a story. How many more stories could it tell?

Where did it come from? Ursula said Mr. Warden, a part-time photographer in Quesnel, gave the desk to Pa-pah. They had worked together on the Grand Trunk Railroad, and when the job finished at Tête Jaune Cache in 1908, they returned to Quesnel together. Ursula said that after Pa-pah opened his store in 1913, Mr. Warden gave him the desk in exchange for groceries.

And if the desk could talk, might it say that Mr. Warden inspired my father in the craft of photography? I wonder. My father noted in his journal that he taught himself photography in Barkerville in 1909 when the gold mines closed in winter and he was in dire need of an income. Today my father's exquisite portraits of Chinese immigrants, First Nations families and Caucasian settlers from the Barkerville and Quesnel area are a tribute to the past.

Who made the desk? Was it an import? Where did the few nicks and scratches come from? The physical condition of the desk hints of untold stories, but what about the stories within its inner sanctum? I speculated and mused over these questions. I wish I'd had the foresight to question my father and his colleagues about their early lives. But I had no interest in the desk or its owners back then. I was too busy, too preoccupied with my own young life to stop and consider what had gone on before.

Now, in my senior years, I appreciate the desk's significance. Like a phantom, it appeared before me in my friend's house and drew me forward with a challenge to rediscover the past. The desk holds many secrets, many stories, and if I listen closely, I will hear them.

As I imagine my father brushing a letter home to China, I find myself at the same desk, scribbling my stories. I like to think that the desk is shaping my thoughts, turning back the pages of time, to pull me into the Hoy Built house and its environs so long ago. I know the desk holds stories beyond my time. Perhaps I am not meant to discover them yet. Is this why a humble piece of furniture returned to me? It must be.

Lily Hoy Price, Star Chew, Lona Joe, Rose Reardon, May Sing, Marline (Mooney) Liu, Avaline Sing. (Missing from the photo is Yvonne Wong.)

Photography Credits

page vi: Hoy Family Collection

page x: P-1801 Barkerville Historic Town Archives.
Acc. #1990.3.1008 [C.D. Hoy Collection]

page 7: Hoy Family Collection

page 12: Hoy Family Collection

page 16: Hoy Family Collection

page 22: P-1601 Barkerville Historic Town Archives.
Acc. #1990.3.482 [C.D. Hoy Collection]

page 27: Hoy Family Collection

page 32: Hoy Family Collection

page 40: Hoy Family Collection

page 50: Hoy Family Collection

page 66: Hoy Family Collection

page 71: Hoy Family Collection

page 74: P-1994.113.8 Quesnel and District Museum and
Archives. Photograph possibly by Reg Booth, used with
permission of his family.

page 82: Hoy Family Collection

page 96: Hoy Family Collection

Acknowledgments

When I was seventy years old I attended a creative writing course at North Island College, Comox Branch, Vancouver Island. I thought it might be fun to learn something about writing, and perhaps it would teach me how to write the stories that swirled about in the back of my mind. In one of the assigned writing exercises I wrote about a pair of shoes from my childhood. A few years later, at the Victoria School of Writing, I submitted the story, "Almost Cinderella," to my teacher and editor Professor Lynne Van Luven. With her encouragement, it was published in *Ricepaper* magazine, and a slightly altered version appears in this book. My family and friends, my editor and writers' groups spurred me on to write more stories.

As I explored my past, stories and incidents, long forgotten, began to emerge. I came to realize what a unique family I had, and what a unique era I had witnessed. I wanted to preserve the stories of my family members, share the experience of growing up in Quesnel in the 1930s, 1940s and 1950s—and describe the influence of my family and my community upon my life.

My memory served me well, but I turned to others for help. I interviewed my sisters and friends, read books and newspapers and studied my father's journal to ensure the authenticity of my work. I wrote these stories for myself, for my children, and for all those who want a peek into the past.

I am grateful and indebted to many people who helped me with this book. I was blessed to meet Lynne Van Luven, who amiably guided me through the intricacies and technicalities of creative writing. I am truly indebted to her for encouraging me to write this book. Thank you, Lynne, for believing in me and thank you, too, for all those email hugs that sustained me throughout the good and bad times.

My sisters, Avaline, May, Rose, Lona, Star and Marline (Mooney), shared their photographs and kindly allowed me to interview them. These sessions triggered memories that brought hours of laughter as well as a tear or two. And a special thanks to Lona who compiled our father's narrative, "History of Chow Dong Hoy" into a journal format. It has been a most useful and authentic source of information. Thank you, dear sisters, for being there for me.

My children, Kent, Tova and Paris, encouraged me to tell my stories because they wanted to hear what my life was like in the old days. Thank you, kids. Your teasing spurred me on!

My friends Margaret Morrow and Marilyn Baker from Nova Scotia fed me lobster as they listened intently to my stories. My niece Linda Cable insisted, "Go for it!" Thank you for reading my manuscript with a critical eye, fine-tuning the text and offering moral support, friendship and love I'll never forget. As I worked on this project, Jean Johnston has been a staunch supporter and a true friend. Betty Hill, Patricia and Ron Mattison, Louise Gilbert, Eileen Seale and others waited patiently for this book to appear. The wait is over, and now where's the party?

Kathy and Mike Dunn and Jim Dickson kindly allowed me to use their names in the story about my sister Irene. I also owe my appreciation to Michael Kew, who offered his insights on the life of my brother, Benny.

I would like to thank Bill Quackenbush, curator at the Barkerville Historic Town, Barkerville, BC for answering my questions and offering the use of photos from the Hoy Collection. My gratitude and thanks to Elizabeth Hunter, Museum and Heritage Manager, Quesnel and District Museum and Archives, and Museum Assistant, Leslie Middleton, who graciously researched archival files for appropriate photographs for this book. Your time and efforts are greatly appreciated. I am also grateful to the families of Reg Boothe and H.W. Warden for their permission to republish early photographs of Quesnel. I am also grateful to my colleagues in Valley Women of Words and Comox Valley Writers' Society; I have learned to adapt and grow from your inspirational comments. Susanna MacWilliams introduced me to the craft of writing, and Traci Skuce helped me see the writing on the wall. Thanks to all my teachers for opening up a new world to me.

I am grateful to the authors of several reference books I used to check dates and historical facts to authenticate my stories. I relied on Gordon R. Elliott's *Quesnel: Commercial Centre of the Cariboo Gold Rush*; the *Quesnel Cariboo Observer* and *A Tribute to the Past: Quesnel & Area 1808–1926*; Branwen C. Patenaude's *Because of Gold*, and Faith Moosang's book, *First Son: Portraits by C.D. Hoy*.

And how do I thank the hard-working staff of Brindle & Glass Publishing who graciously welcomed me into their fold? Publisher Ruth Linka took a chance and accepted my manuscript for publication. It made me dance the light fantastic! Emily Shorthouse, Promotions Coordinator, compiled my biography, sorted pictures and gave me a glimpse into what was yet to come. My editor, Linda Goyette, was a godsend. A diligent and gifted editor, she helped me unlock so many doors. When the workload got heavy, she reminded me of the little train engine that said, "I think I can, I think I can. . . ." I laughed and carried on. Her job is no easy task and I thank her for all her kindness and friendship and everything else.

Finally, and most importantly, my husband, Frank, helped me over the hills and across the valleys with patience and understanding. I thank him with love and gratitude. And in my endeavours to become a writer, he became an excellent cook.

Lily Hoy Price
December 2008

Lily Hoy Price grew up in Quesnel, British Columbia and is the ninth daughter of twelve children in the Hoy family. She has lived in England, Nigeria, Uganda and Nova Scotia. Her writing has been published in *Ricepaper* magazine and in the collection of essays, *Verve* (2006). This is her first book. Lily lives in Courtenay, BC.